Dedication

I would like to dedicate this book to all those Christians who are unwilling to accept what others say but are like the Bereans who looked to the Scriptures for the truth: "Now these Jews were more noble than those in Thessalonica; they received the word with all eagerness, examining the Scriptures daily to see if these things were so" (Acts 17:11).

Acknowledgments

I especially want to say "thank you" to my lovely wife, Jan, for all the patience she had with my absence during the study of this project. I would also like to acknowledge those who have lent advice, knowledge, comments, and encouragement over the many years this project has taken to come to fruition. This project has been long with many rewritings, with grammar and punctuation corrections to the manuscript. I say a hearty thank-you for all you have done to make this project a success: Reverend Eugene White, Reverend Ed Parman, Reverend Larry Maddox, Doctor Steven Edmondson, Lance and Kathy Parman, Dave Wisen, and James Maiden.

Contents

Preface. 11
Introduction. 15
1 Scripture Defining Scripture 19
2 Views about the End 23
3 The Wrath of God 29
    What Is the Wrath of God? 29
    Noah and the Flood 30
    Sodom and Gomorrah 33
The Struggle between Good and Evil. 41
4 The Beginning of the Struggle. 43
    The Flood: a Shadow of the End-Time 45
    God Begins His Kingdom 47
    Sodom and Gomorrah:
    Another Shadow of the End-Time 47
5 A Nation is Born. 53
    Israel in Egypt 54
6 Israel and the Assyrians 59
7 Judah and the Babylonians. 63
    Nebuchadnezzar Has a Dream. 65
8 Israel and the Medo-Persian Empire 73
9 Israel and the Grecian Empire 79
10 Israel and the Roman Empire. 85
11 The "Not Yet Come" Empire 93
12 The Fourth Beast Empire. 99
13 Investigating Current End-time Beliefs 121

14 The Last Trumpet........................... 125
15 The Seven-Year Tribulation................... 135
16 The 2,300 Evenings and Mornings 143
17 The Imminence of Christ's Return.............. 151
18 The Book of Revelation....................... 159
19 The Seven Churches......................... 163
20 John Is Called into Heaven 169
21 The Scroll................................. 175
    Understanding the End-Time.................. 175
    The Outside of the Scroll.................... 179
    Who Removed the Seals? 180
22 Seal One. The Deceiver Comes................. 183
23 Seal Two. Wars and Rumors of War 187
24 Seal Three. Famine 189
25 The Middle of the Week...................... 191
    The Great Tribulation....................... 191
    Israel Is Invaded........................... 195
    The Woman and the Dragon 202
    The Dragon Gives the Beast His Authority...... 213
    The False Prophet 214
    The Abomination of Desolation............... 223
    The Two Witnesses 227
26 Seals Four and Five. Death and Martyrdom 237
27 Seal Six. God Announces His Coming
    with the Signs!............................ 241
28 The Rapture and the Wrath 247
    Rapture Does Not Occur until after the Sign..... 256

What Does Jesus Say about
　　the Great Tribulation? 258
29 The Fall of Babylon 261
　　Ancient Babylon 261
　　The United Arab Emirates 278
30 The Rapture 279
　　What Is the Rapture? 280
　　Why Is There a Rapture? 282
　　When and How Does the Rapture Occur? 284
31 Before the Seventh Seal 289
32 Seventh Seal 293
33 God's Wrath 295
34 The Trumpets 303
　　First Judgment 308
　　Second Judgment 309
　　Third Judgment 310
　　Fourth Judgment 311
　　Fifth Judgment 313
　　Sixth Judgment 315
　　The Seven Thunders 318
　　Seventh Judgment 321
35 After the Battle 327
36 Putting the Pieces Together 333
About the Author 341

Preface

The Conflict

It all began before the foundations of the world were put in place. Satan decided in his heart that he was going to take over God's kingdom. When God created mankind and placed Adam and Eve in a garden called Eden with the purpose of taking care of planet Earth, Satan realized that mankind would be his pathway to achieving his goal. He would seduce mankind with deceit.

In this garden, God placed a man and a woman. They were to serve and obey Him. There was, however, this problem that had arisen in heaven where God's creation spun the entire universe. He had created others for the purpose of helping Him govern the stars, planets, and constellations; they were called angels. Angels were created with varying degrees of authority; their purpose was to worship God by their service and utter obedience to Him. Their duties demanded that angels have the intelligence to make decisions on their own. So, they were endowed with the *power of choice*.

The power of choice is the power to obey God or to disobey Him. To obey would bring blessings, but to disobey would bring consequences.

God created millions of these angelic beings to assist Him in His creation. He created some as leaders who would oversee others. Lucifer was one of these angelic beings, with authority over a multitude of angels in the angelic order. He was created with a beauty so astounding that he would become proud of his looks and ability to rule others. Lucifer decided to rebel against God and take over His kingdom.

He convinced the angels under his control to follow him in rebellion, which was about one-third of the angels God had created. Heaven was the battleground until God placed a new creation with authority over planet Earth. He knew, however, that Lucifer would intervene in His plans and interrupt the workings. So God placed in the garden a tree called "the tree of the knowledge of good and evil." He gave mankind two commandments:

1. Take care of the Garden ("thou shalt").
2. Do not eat of the tree of the knowledge of good and evil ("thou shalt not").

He told them the consequence of choosing to eat the fruit of this tree: "In the day that thou eatest thereof thou shalt surely die" (Genesis 2:17, KJV).

Lucifer deceived one-third of the angelic host into following him, and he believed he would also be able to deceive man. He wanted to use the earth as a battleground for his ulterior motive of usurping God's power and authority. His goal was to take over God's kingdom and be worshiped as the ultimate authority of all creation.

Lucifer felt that if he could convince Adam and Eve to eat of the fruit of the tree of the knowledge of good and evil through deceit, he would have defeated God, and his first victory would be to take over the dominion of the planet Earth.

> *And the LORD God commanded the man, saying, Of every tree of the garden thou mayest freely eat: But of the tree of the knowledge of good and evil, thou shalt not eat of it: for in the day that thou eatest thereof thou shalt surely die.*
> **Genesis 2:16–17 (KJV)**

Adam and Eve, created in God's image, were, in some respect, like God. Now Satan comes along, and in his attempt to usurp God's authority with his deceitfulness, he emphasizes *every tree* instead of just one.

> *Now the serpent was more subtil than any beast of the field which the LORD God had made. And he said unto the woman, Yea, hath God said, Ye shall not eat of every tree of the garden?*
> **Genesis 3:1 (KJV)**

A subtle lie leading to the next subtle lie. Satan's first lie is designed to lure Eve into a conversation with him that he would be able to control; Eve takes the bait and is now in a dialog with Satan that she would not win. His next lie is, "Ye shall not surely die" (Genesis 3:4, KJV).

Satan placed the idea in Eve's mind that God had lied to Adam and her. Now Eve was hooked. All Satan had to do was reel in his catch. Satan took dominion over God's crowning achievement. Mankind was now under satanic influence, and with it came dominion over planet Earth. Man sold his birthright to Satan for the fruit of the forbidden tree.

Now God would expel man from the garden He had provided. As a result, Adam and Eve lost access to not only the tree of life but all the trees God had provided for them.

It is as if Adam and Eve said, "We want to be like God."

God, however, provided a *plan of escape* for man, but man would have to choose to escape Satan's bondage. As Satan would be unwilling to release his slaves without a fight, so began the struggle.

God put in place a plan of redemption for man. Through man's redemption, God would defeat Lucifer and, eventually, send him to his eternal punishment, the lake of fire.

The conflict continues.

Introduction

I once bought a puzzle with a nice picture on the front of the box, took it home, opened the box, and dumped 500 pieces on the table. Some were the right side up; some showed the back. The first thing needing to be done was to put the right side of the pieces up and lay them out on a flat table with no pieces on top of another.

Next, the pieces needed to be sorted into what seemed to be a logical color scheme. I then took all edge pieces and arranged them likewise. Now I was ready to begin assembling the pieces together. There was no way to look at the individual pieces and imagine what that picture would be when all the pieces were together.

In looking at some of the same-colored pieces, I noticed it seemed as if they would fit but did not. They were close, but on examination, I discovered they did not fit. I had to look further.

Soon, enthusiasm turned into frustration. I set the puzzle aside to pick up later when there was more time and nothing else to do. What I thought would be a quick evening of relaxation turned into disappointment.

When I finally finished the puzzle, it looked exactly like the picture on the front of the box.

There is another box with a puzzle in it. It has thousands of pieces. It has the most beautiful picture when completed. Only one challenge: there's no picture on the front of the box. We must put the pieces together to see the real picture. Another challenge is that the box has other pieces that go into other pictures. Great! Now we need to decide which of the pictures we want to put together and sort those pieces accordingly.

The puzzle called *the Bible* contains pictures of creation, the fall of man, God's law, His Son, Jesus, of redemption, of heaven, of Christ's return to the earth to put an end to evil, and a puzzle for almost any subject imaginable.

An attempt to assemble the picture of the end-time uncovers the pieces intertwined with other pictures hidden in the Bible.

In the Bible, we find sixty-six books telling the story of God's dealing with mankind, what He did, what He is doing, and what He is going to do. We need to read it prayerfully to understand what He is saying. We see a bit of the story here and a bit there throughout all the books of the Bible.

To see what the picture looks like, we must *ask*, *seek*, *find*, and *pray*.

When reading books written by men about the end-time, we find these books will give us different views. They all claim to have the *truth* concerning the picture. So, we need to act like the Bereans, the Jews referred to by Paul in Acts 17:11 saying, "Now these Jews were more noble than those in Thessalonica; they received the word with all eagerness, examining the Scriptures daily to see if these things were so."

Introduction

These Bereans liked what Paul was saying but wanted scriptural proof that what he was claiming was true.

Likewise, in our search of the Scriptures to test if scholars' claims were true, we find errors in some of their ideas, concepts, and assumptions concerning the end-time.

We find some have put pieces in the wrong place, which distorts the picture. If they have put a piece in the wrong place, that piece is no longer available to be put in the correct place, so the overall picture is distorted.

When working on God's puzzle, we must look at it without preconceived ideas. We must let God's Word tell us where each piece belongs, not where someone wants to put it.

I tried to look only at what Scripture has to say and not what someone's opinion was. The Scriptures hold the pieces necessary to get the right picture. As a result, I took the position to let *Scripture speak for itself.*

I trust this effort will not be my opinion but a search for the truth of what the Scriptures have to say about the end-time. During this study, I have had to change some of my understanding of what the Scriptures are saying. I trust you also will allow the Scriptures to speak for themselves.

It is extremely beneficial for this study that you read all indicated scriptures. Most all pertinent scriptures have been inserted into the text. However, there are some portions of Scripture omitted because of their length. It is extremely crucial those scriptures also be read, as this book is *letting Scripture tell us the story of the end.*

Please have a Bible handy as you read.

Italicized Scripture

In this book you will find many Scriptures given to present what they have to say concerning the various subjects. Most all italicized Scripture will be that of the author to emphasize the thoughts presented.

1
Scripture Defining Scripture

People today desire to understand biblical events such as prophecy, end-time, the Great Tribulation, the rapture, and God's wrath.

Much has been preached and written concerning this end. Movies and TV programs concerning the apocalypse, the four horsemen, the Antichrist, the Mayan calendar, etc., are nothing more than man's assumption of what it means or how it might happen.

The subject is ripe for deception. Jesus warned us in Matthew 24:4–5, 24 (KJV) about this possibility:

> *And Jesus answered and said unto them, Take heed that no man deceive you. For many shall come in my name, saying, I am Christ; and shall deceive many. [...] For there shall arise false Christs, and false prophets, and shall show great signs and wonders; insomuch that, if it were possible, they shall deceive the very elect.*

Also, in Mark 13:5–6 (KJV), we read: "And Jesus answering them began to say, Take heed lest any man *deceive* you: For many shall come in my name, saying, I am Christ; and shall *deceive* many." And in Ephesians 5:6 (KJV): "Let no man *deceive* you with vain words: for because of these things cometh the wrath of God upon the children of disobedience."

Moreover, Paul writes in 2 Thessalonians 2:1–3 (KJV),

> *Now we beseech you, brethren, by the coming of our Lord Jesus Christ, and by our gathering together unto him, That ye be not soon shaken in mind, or be troubled, neither by spirit, nor by word, nor by letter as from us, as that the day of Christ is at hand. Let no man deceive you by any means: for that day shall not come, except there come a falling away first, and that man of sin be revealed, the son of perdition.*

So, the Bible has warned us about the possibility of deception regarding this end-time. Deception is extremely prevalent in the writings about the final seven years of history before Christ returns to set up His kingdom on the earth. I do not believe it is intentional because it is what some believe.

There are many writings about the rapture, featuring different interpretations, so it is very easy to be deceived, but Revelation 1:3 (KJV) tells us: "Blessed is he that readeth, and they that hear the words of this prophecy, and keep those things which are written therein: for the time is at hand."

Scripture Defining Scripture

Also, in Revelation 22:7 (KJV), it is written: "Behold, I come quickly: blessed is he that keepeth the sayings of the prophecy of this book."

POINTS TO PONDER

1. Why should I let Scripture speak for itself?
2. What can I do to know the truth about a scriptural subject?

2
Views about the End

Amillennialism is a belief that there is no difference between the church and Israel. The kingdom of God is now present, and there is no literal millennial kingdom. Both the righteous and the wicked are resurrected at the same time, followed by a general judgment.

Postmillennialism is a belief that the gospel will bring us into the millennial age. We will experience tribulation in this present age, but the gospel of Jesus Christ will prevail, as a majority will accept Christ and be saved. There will be one rapture of both the righteous and the wicked at the end of the millennial period. Then comes the judgment for all.

Premillennialism is a belief that there will be a literal return of Christ, after which He will set up His 1,000-year kingdom of peace. There are varying views within this camp as to the order of events preceding Christ's literal "kingdom of God." Within this belief lie four views of Daniel's seventieth-week prophecy of Daniel 9:24–27:

1. Pre-Tribulation View

The view that the rapture of the church could happen at any moment, that it is secret and happens before the seal openings of Revelation 6. The rapture also occurs before the beginning of Daniel's seventieth week, as they believe that Daniel's prophecy is for the Jews only.

2. Mid-Tribulation View

The view that the church will experience the first half (three and a half years) of Daniel's seventieth-week prophecy and be raptured at the midpoint of the seventieth week.

3. Post-Tribulation View

The view that the church will experience all events of Daniel's seventieth-week prophecy and be subject to God's wrath before being raptured at Christ's second coming at the end of the seventieth week.

4. Pre-Wrath View

The view that the church will experience the events of Daniel's seventieth week up to the time God begins to pour out His wrath. The view is that we are not exempt from Satan's wrath but are exempt from God's wrath.

Within each of these four views are differences of opinion. These statements are not intended to indicate the full belief of each but just a general overview.

Views about the End

All seem to have a measure of truth to support their view. Do these views have the Gospel truth about the rapture of the church and the events leading up to it, or are they just assumptions? Unless they have scriptural support for their position, they are just assumptions.

There have been many books written concerning the end-time and the timing of the rapture. The analysis of the scriptures ranges all over the place. Some say the rapture is before the seventieth week of Daniel's prophecy. Others say the rapture will take place in the middle of the week; some believe the rapture is at the end, and others believe it is just before God's wrath. Some say it does not happen until the end of the 1,000-year millennial reign of Christ. Still, others say there are at least two raptures. Some say three. Who is right?

Even within each of these positions, there is still no 100 percent agreement.

It is my goal to let Scripture tell us when the events associated with Christ's return for His church will take place. For us to be objective and unbiased, we must set aside our own notions, beliefs, and assumptions concerning these events.

Is there a reason for the inconsistency of understanding about this last seven-year period in history? I believe there is. Daniel was told the following in his vision recorded in Daniel 12:9 (KJV): "And he said, Go thy way, Daniel: for the words are closed up and sealed till the time of the end."

I believe we are now living in the end-time, as many of these prophecies are beginning to be understood.

Also, Jesus spoke in parables to reveal the truth to those who were ready in their hearts to receive it. Satan was and is the master deceiver. He wants to deceive you. So, it is extremely important we have a correct understanding of the Scriptures.

One reason the end-time is misunderstood is that information about it is found throughout all of Scripture. It is like a puzzle. We must find the pieces and put them in the proper place.

The purpose of this book is not to use other authors' words or opinions and accept them as Gospel but to be like the Bereans relying on the scriptures to determine what is true.

> *The brothers immediately sent Paul and Silas away by night to Berea, and when they arrived they went into the Jewish synagogue. Now these Jews were more noble than those in Thessalonica; they received the word with all eagerness, examining the Scriptures daily to see if these things were so.*
> **Acts 17:10–11**

Therefore, my goal will be to look at Scripture only. We will let Scripture speak for itself. As for information not in Scripture, we will look at evidence of fulfilled prophecy since biblical times, such as the reestablishment of the Israelite nation.

So, let us see if we can sort out the pieces of Scripture and put them in the right place. Second Timothy 2:15 (KJV) tells us to "study to show thyself approved unto God, a workman that needeth not to be ashamed, *rightly dividing the word of truth.*"

I believe it means Scripture is to be understood in the context in which it is given. We should not take it out of context to apply it to what we think it should mean. Second Timothy 3:16–17 (KJV) says,

> *All scripture is given by inspiration of God, and is profitable for doctrine, for reproof, for correction, for instruction in righteousness: That the man of God may be perfect, thoroughly furnished unto all good works.*

A good rule of thumb concerning Scripture is: *if the plain sense makes sense, it's the right sense*, so don't try to change it. So, do not try to make Scripture say something it does not.

We will find, if we are diligent to search the scriptures, that they have all the answers to the knowledge we seek.

POINTS TO PONDER

1. Why are there so many views about the end?
2. Where do I place my view?
3. Why do I believe it is right?

3
The Wrath of God

Much has been said and written about the four horsemen. Some seem to equate this with God's wrath, but is it? We will understand, as we go through our study, that the four horsemen represent not God's wrath but Satan's, as he knows his time is short.

What Is the Wrath of God?

There are thirteen Hebrew words and four Greek words in the New Testament translated into the English language as "wrath." All are not necessarily referring to the wrath occurring during the end-time. Some are referring to an individual's wrath against another. Others are referring to one nation against another. Even when it is referring to God, it is not necessarily the wrath concerning the end-time. God's end-time wrath is normally referred to as "the day of the Lord." The phrase "in that day" is also used many times to refer to God's time of wrath.

There are some whose viewpoint looks at this last week of Daniel's prophecy as when God again turns His focus upon Israel. In doing so, He shows His dealings with the church are over, so He *raptures* them. They look at this last seven-year period as God's wrath, but is it?

When God's wrath is poured out during the end-time, *God alone will be exalted.* Satan seems to be having his way with the first portion of this last week, but when God's wrath is poured out, it is evident "the Lord alone will be exalted in that day," as Isaiah 2:11 declares: "The haughty looks of man shall be brought low, and the lofty pride of men shall be humbled, and *the Lord alone will be exalted in that day.*"

God's wrath in the Bible is not always associated with the utter destruction of evil. It may be used as a time of judgment upon His people. We must then understand what the term "wrath" means: judgment designed to bring His people back to Him or designed to annihilate evil.

In the case of the end-time, we see God's wrath is directed against evil. It is "the day of the Lord" or similar words denoting God's wrath at the time of the end.

Jesus gives us events to look at concerning the end-time and wrath. Matthew 24:37 and Luke 17:26–27 tell us to look at Noah and look at Sodom and Gomorrah in Luke 17:28–30. Let's look at these two events to see if there is information we can glean concerning these events before and during the outpouring of God's wrath at the end-time.

Noah and the Flood

> Then the Lord said, "My Spirit shall not abide in man forever, for he is flesh: his days shall be

The Wrath of God

> *120 years." The Nephilim were on the earth in those days, and also afterward, when the sons of God came in to the daughters of man and they bore children to them. These were the mighty men who were of old, the men of renown. The LORD saw that the wickedness of man was great in the earth, and that every intention of the thoughts of his heart was only evil continually. And the LORD was sorry that he had made man on the earth, and it grieved him to his heart. So the LORD said, "I will blot out man whom I have created from the face of the land, man and animals and creeping things and birds of the heavens, for I am sorry that I have made them." But Noah found favor in the eyes of the LORD.*
>
> **Genesis 6:3–8**

God allowed mankind to live for 120 years and told Noah to build an ark because *He was going to destroy mankind because of their wickedness.*

> *Then the LORD said to Noah, "Go into the ark, you and all your household, for I have seen that you are righteous before me in this generation. Take with you seven pairs of all clean animals, the male and his mate, and a pair of the animals that are not clean, the male and his mate, and seven pairs of the birds of the heavens also, male and female, to keep their offspring alive on the face of all the earth. For in seven days I will send rain on the earth forty days and forty nights,*

and every living thing that I have made I will blot out from the face of the ground." And Noah did all that the LORD had commanded him. Noah was six hundred years old when the flood of waters came upon the earth. And Noah and his sons and his wife and his sons' wives with him went into the ark to escape the waters of the flood. Of clean animals, and of animals that are not clean, and of birds, and of everything that creeps on the ground, two and two, male and female, went into the ark with Noah, as God had commanded Noah. And after seven days the waters of the flood came upon the earth. In the six hundredth year of Noah's life, in the second month, on the seventeenth day of the month, on that day all the fountains of the great deep burst forth, and the windows of the heavens were opened. And rain fell upon the earth forty days and forty nights. On the very same day Noah and his sons, Shem and Ham and Japheth, and Noah's wife and the three wives of his sons with them entered the ark, they and every beast, according to its kind, and all the livestock according to their kinds, and every creeping thing that creeps on the earth, according to its kind, and every bird, according to its kind, every winged creature. They went into the ark with Noah, two and two of all flesh in which there was the breath of life. And those that entered, male and female of all flesh, went in as God had commanded him. And the LORD shut him in.

Genesis 7:1–16

The Wrath of God

What things can we understand about Noah and the flood, and how does it give us information concerning God's wrath during the end-time?

- God saw the people were evil (evil had infested the earth), and He regretted that He had made humanity, "but Noah found favor" (Genesis 6:3–8).
- God told Noah to take his family and the animals into the ark to protect them for the future population of the earth (God would provide protection for the righteous) (Genesis 7:2–3).
- Noah and his family entered the ark on *the same day the floods came*, and the Lord shut the door (Genesis 7:4–13).

Once the flood began, admittance into the ark *was denied*, for God had shut the door.

Sodom and Gomorrah

> *Then the LORD said, "Because the outcry against Sodom and Gomorrah is great and their sin is very grave, I will go down to see whether they have done altogether according to the outcry that has come to me. And if not, I will know."*
>
> **Genesis 18:20–21**

> *The two angels came to Sodom in the evening, and Lot was sitting in the gate of Sodom. When Lot saw them, he rose to meet them and bowed himself with his face to the Earth and said, "My lords, please turn aside to your*

servant's house and spend the night and wash your feet. Then you may rise up early and go on your way." They said, "No; we will spend the night in the town square." But he pressed them strongly; so they turned aside to him and entered his house. And he made them a feast and baked unleavened bread, and they ate. But before they lay down, the men of the city, the men of Sodom, both young and old, all the people to the last man, surrounded the house. And they called to Lot, "Where are the men who came to you tonight? Bring them out to us, that we may know them." Lot went out to the men at the entrance, shut the door after him, and said, "I beg you, my brothers, do not act so wickedly. Behold, I have two daughters who have not known any man. Let me bring them out to you, and do to them as you please. Only do nothing to these men, for they have come under the shelter of my roof." But they said, "Stand back!" And they said, "This fellow came to sojourn, and he has become the judge! Now we will deal worse with you than with them." Then they pressed hard against the man Lot, and drew near to break the door down. But the men reached out their hands and brought Lot into the house with them and shut the door. And they struck with blindness the men who were at the entrance of the house, both small and great, so that they wore themselves out groping for the door. Then the men said to Lot, "Have you anyone else here? Sons-in-law, sons, daughters, or anyone you have in the city, bring them out of the place. For we are about to destroy this place, because the outcry against its people has become great before the L*ORD, and the* L*ORD has sent us to destroy it." So Lot went out and said to his sons-in-law, who were to marry his daughters, "Up! Get out of this place, for the* L*ORD is about to destroy the city." But he seemed to his sons-in-law to be jesting. As morning dawned, the angels urged Lot, saying, "Up! Take your wife and your two daughters who are here, lest you be swept away in the punishment of the city." But he lingered. So the men seized him and his wife and his two daughters by the hand, the* L*ORD being merciful to him, and they brought him out and set him outside the city. And as they brought them out, one said, "Escape for your life. Do not look back or stop anywhere in the valley. Escape to the hills, lest you be swept away." And Lot said to them, "Oh, no, my lords. Behold, your servant has found favor in your sight, and you have shown me great kindness in saving my life. But I cannot escape to the hills, lest the disaster overtake me and I die. Behold, this city is near enough to flee to, and it is a little one. Let me escape there—is it not a little one?—and my life will be saved!" He said to him, "Behold, I grant you this favor also, that I will not overthrow the city of which you have spoken. Escape there quickly, for I can do nothing till you arrive there." Therefore the name of the city was called Zoar. The sun had risen on the Earth when Lot came*

God's End-Time Puzzle

*to Zoar. Then the L*ORD *rained on Sodom and Gomorrah sulfur and fire from the L*ORD *out of heaven. And he overthrew those cities, and all the valley, and all the inhabitants of the cities, and what grew on the ground. But Lot's wife, behind him, looked back, and she became a pillar of salt. And Abraham went early in the morning to the place where he had stood before the L*ORD*. And he looked down toward Sodom and Gomorrah and toward all the land of the valley, and he looked and, behold, the smoke of the land went up like the smoke of a furnace.*

Genesis 19:1–28

Here is what we can understand about Sodom and Gomorrah.

- They were evil-minded individuals (the cities were infested with evil). See Genesis 18:20–21.
- They were sexually immoral (Genesis 19:4–5).
- God sent wrath upon them to destroy them (Genesis 19:24).
- Lot, his wife, and two daughters were led to safety (God provided protection for the righteous) (Genesis 19:16–17).
- Lot's wife desired to go back and was destroyed (Genesis 19:26).
- On the *same day* Lot left, the cities were destroyed (Genesis 19:22–24).

Both events show us three things:

1. God delivers the righteous from His wrath.

The Wrath of God

2. The destruction begins on the *same day* the righteous are delivered.
3. No deliverance was available to those under God's wrath.

Jesus told us to look at these two events and then told us the end will be just like these two events.

What can we ascertain?

- The church (redeemed individuals) will be protected (raptured) before this period of God's wrath.
- God will destroy the evil of the earth.
- No deliverance will be available once God's wrath begins.
- The deliverance of the church will happen on the *same day* God's wrath begins.

All this is evidence that God's judgment is right, and as a result you will be counted worthy of the kingdom of God, for which you are suffering. God is just: He will pay back trouble to those who trouble you and give relief to you who are troubled, and to us as well. This will happen when the Lord Jesus is revealed from heaven in blazing fire with his powerful angels. He will punish those who do not know God and do not obey the gospel of our Lord Jesus. They will be punished with everlasting destruction and shut out from the presence of the Lord and from the glory of his might on the day he comes to be glorified in his holy people and to be marveled at among

> *all those who have believed. This includes you, because you believed our testimony to you. With this in mind, we constantly pray for you, that our God may make you worthy of his calling, and that by his power he may bring to fruition your every desire for goodness and your every deed prompted by faith. We pray this so that the name of our Lord Jesus may be glorified in you, and you in him, according to the grace of our God and the Lord Jesus Christ.*
>
> **2 Thessalonians 1:5–12 (NIV)**

Please note that the two incidents where God poured out His wrath were different in only one respect. One was worldwide and one local. The intent was the same: to destroy wickedness. In looking at God's wrath during the end-time, we understand His wrath can be both worldwide and localized.

So now, can these conclusions be supported concerning the events of the end-time? I believe they can. Let's look at what Scripture tells us about the events of the end-time.

Let's start by looking at the struggle between good and evil, keeping in mind the evidence obtained from studying the stories of Noah and Lot.

First, let us say there are several opinions and assumptions concerning the end-time that are preached as Gospel truth. They cannot all be Gospel truth. All seem to have some truth, but not necessarily all the truth.

In addressing these assumptions, we must look further

into the Scriptures. Assumptions can be devastating to understanding Scripture. In our diligent study of Scripture concerning the end-time, let's agree to throw out our assumptions and let Scripture alone inform us.

POINTS TO PONDER

1. What is the wrath of God?
2. When does God's wrath, "the Lord's day," begin?
3. What happens on the first day of God's wrath?
4. Why did Jesus tell us to look at Noah and Lot?

The Struggle between Good and Evil

There is some redundancy in this section, as the pieces of this portion of the puzzle are interrelated. It will help solidify in your mind the complexity of this information.

4

The Beginning of the Struggle

The struggle between good and evil began before the foundations of the earth were put in place. Satan rebelled, desiring to defeat God and take over His creation as recorded in Isaiah 14:12–15:

> *How you are fallen from heaven, O Day Star, son of Dawn! How you are cut down to the ground, you who laid the nations low! You said in your heart,*
>
> *"I will ascend to heaven; above the stars of God I will set my throne on high;*
>
> *I will sit on the mount of assembly in the far reaches of the north;*
>
> *I will ascend above the heights of the clouds;*
>
> *I will make myself like the Most High."*

But you are brought down to Sheol, to the far reaches of the pit.

God put in place a plan of redemption for His ultimate creation, as He knew man would succumb to the wiles of Satan. The struggle began in the Garden of Eden when Satan entered the scene using a serpent as his disguise. His diabolical scheme began with deception, and deception would be his trademark throughout the rest of human history.

At this point, God declared a curse upon Satan, saying the seed of the woman would bruise the head of Satan while Satan would bruise the heel of her seed; the seed of the woman would be Jesus.

> *The LORD God said to the serpent, "Because you have done this, cursed are you above all livestock and above all beasts of the field; on your belly you shall go, and dust you shall eat all the days of your life. I will put enmity between you and the woman, and between your offspring and her offspring; he shall bruise your head, and you shall bruise his heel."*
>
> **Genesis 3:14–15**

Evil seemed to dominate until God destroyed humanity with a flood. Noah, however, found grace in the eyes of the Lord and was spared, along with his wife, three sons, and their wives.

There is no evidence of any government entities, so anarchy likely ruled. Tribes and clans, most likely, would have banded together in small communities for survival, but nothing on the scale of nation-building.

The Flood: a Shadow of the End-Time

Jesus, in Matthew 24:36–39, tells us,

> *But concerning that day and hour no one knows, not even the angels of heaven, nor the Son, but the Father only. For as were the days of Noah, so will be the coming of the Son of Man. For as in those days before the flood they were eating and drinking, marrying and giving in marriage, until the day when Noah entered the ark, and they were unaware until the flood came and swept them all away, so will be the coming of the Son of Man.*

Jesus is telling us to look closely at the days of Noah to understand what it will be like when the "Son of Man" (Jesus) returns to pour out His wrath upon humanity. In reading the story of Noah in Genesis, chapters six and seven, we find:

- God gave Noah the warning seven days in advance (Genesis 7:4).
- Wrath begins (Genesis 7:11).
- The door of the ark was shut *on the day* wrath began (Genesis 7:13).
- The Lord shut Noah in (Genesis 7:16).

It was not long after the flood that evil again began to show its ugly face. Nimrod, the great-grandson of Noah through Ham, his youngest son, built Babylon, where the

Tower of Babel is believed to have been built. It was there that God confused their language.

> *Now the whole Earth had one language and the same words. And as people migrated from the east, they found a plain in the land of Shinar and settled there. And they said to one another, "Come, let us make bricks, and burn them thoroughly." And they had brick for stone, and bitumen for mortar. Then they said, "Come, let us build ourselves a city and a tower with its top in the heavens, and let us make a name for ourselves, lest we be dispersed over the face of the whole Earth." And the LORD came down to see the city and the tower, which the children of man had built. And the LORD said, "Behold, they are one people, and they have all one language, and this is only the beginning of what they will do. And nothing that they propose to do will now be impossible for them. Come, let us go down and there confuse their language, so that they may not understand one another's speech." So the LORD dispersed them from there over the face of all the Earth, and they left off building the city. Therefore its name was called Babel, because there the LORD confused the language of all the Earth. And from there the LORD dispersed them over the face of all the Earth.*
>
> **Genesis 11:1–9**

The Beginning of the Struggle

Babylon was one of the first centers of Nimrod's kingdom. Following the dispersion, he eventually built Nineveh, along with other cities. These two cities would play important roles in Satan's effort to destroy God's people. Nineveh would become the seat of the Assyrian Empire, and Babylon—the seat of the Babylonian Empire.

God Begins His Kingdom

Abram, whose name God later changed to Abraham (we will refer to him as *Abraham*), was born about 292 years after the flood, according to biblical chronology (which is debated). God would call him to leave Ur of the Chaldeans for the purpose of establishing a people for Himself (see Acts 7:1–4).

Ur, an important city in the time of Abraham, was heavily involved in idolatrous worship. It is in this setting God revealed Himself to Abraham and called him to a land He would show him (Genesis 12:1). God required this departure to separate Abraham from the influences of idol worship. Once Abraham was separated, God was able to deal with him in a personal way.

Sodom and Gomorrah: Another Shadow of the End-Time

It was during Abraham's day, before the time of Isaac, that Lot, Abraham's nephew, moved to the well-watered plains because of a conflict between Abraham's livestock servants and those of Lot. Eventually, Lot moved his family into Sodom, a wicked city where its inhabitants practiced sexual deviation.

God announced to Abraham that He would destroy the cities of the plains because of their wickedness. Abraham pleaded with God's messengers for mercy on the cities if ten righteous could be found. They agreed, but they could not find ten righteous souls. So, the messengers led Lot, his wife, and two daughters to safety before God destroyed the cities (Genesis 18:17–22).

- Only Lot and his family were saved; his wife, however, looked back and was turned into a pillar of salt (Genesis 19:26).
- The cities were destroyed on the *same day* Lot departed (Genesis 19:23, Luke 17:29).

Jesus said in Luke 17:25–30,

> *But first he must suffer many things and be rejected by this generation. Just as it was in the days of Noah, so will it be in the days of the Son of Man. They were eating and drinking and marrying and being given in marriage, until the day when Noah entered the ark, and the flood came and destroyed them all. Likewise, just as it was in the days of Lot—they were eating and drinking, buying and selling, planting and building, but on the day when Lot went out from Sodom, fire and sulfur rained from heaven and destroyed them all—so will it be on the day when the Son of Man is revealed.*

God continues to deal with Abraham to build the nation of Israel.

The Beginning of the Struggle

Isaac, Abraham's son through his wife, Sarah, was the father of Jacob, whose twelve sons became the twelve tribes of Israel.

In Genesis 37:9–11, we find Joseph, the first son of Jacob's wife, Rachel, receiving a dream; he was also Jacob's favorite son.

> *Then he dreamed another dream and told it to his brothers and said, "Behold, I have dreamed another dream. Behold, the sun, the moon, and eleven stars were bowing down to me." But when he told it to his father and to his brothers, his father rebuked him and said to him, "What is this dream that you have dreamed? Shall I and your mother and your brothers indeed come to bow ourselves to the ground before you?" And his brothers were jealous of him, but his father kept the saying in mind.*

The book of Revelation shows a similar vision received by John, revealing a serpent with seven heads, ten horns, and seven crowns. We see *a great red dragon* standing ready to devour the child who should be born from the woman.

> *And a great sign appeared in heaven: a woman clothed with the sun, with the moon under her feet, and on her head a crown of twelve stars. [Remember Joseph's dream.] She was pregnant and was crying out in birth pains and the agony of giving birth. And another sign appeared in heaven: behold, a*

great red dragon, with seven heads and ten horns, and on his heads seven diadems. His tail swept down a third of the stars of heaven and cast them to the Earth. And the dragon stood before the woman who was about to give birth, so that when she bore her child he might devour it. She gave birth to a male child, one who is to rule all the nations with a rod of iron, but her child was caught up to God and to his throne, and the woman fled into the wilderness, where she has a place prepared by God, in which she is to be nourished for 1,260 days. Now war arose in heaven, Michael and his angels fighting against the dragon. And the dragon and his angels fought back, but he was defeated, and there was no longer any place for them in heaven. And the great dragon was thrown down, that ancient serpent, who is called the devil and Satan, the deceiver of the whole world—he was thrown down to the Earth, and his angels were thrown down with him.

Revelation 12:1–9
(hereinafter, the text in brackets mine)

So, what can we understand from this portion of Scripture?

First, God is revealing to John this struggle between the forces of good and evil that goes way back to a time when God was beginning to establish a people for Himself. Actually, all the way back to Adam and Eve in the Garden of Eden. However, God destroyed the evil with the flood. Noah built an ark to save his family along with a few of

The Beginning of the Struggle

every species of birds and animals. God started over with Noah and his family.

Second, God reveals that this struggle involves Israel and Christians, the woman (Israel) and the Son (Jesus who established Christianity).

We now understand that the serpent, even at the time of Jacob, knew the Redeemer of mankind would come from the lineage of Jacob. He would do all in his power to thwart God's plan. Satan's assault began with Jacob's family, even though they were but seventy souls who would go into Egypt. The serpent was none other than Satan. We see a pattern beginning with Satan disrupting God's plan in the Garden of Eden. Again, we see evidence that Satan is trying to foil God's plan for establishing a godly people.

If you are unfamiliar with the early history of the Jewish people, read Genesis 37 and 39–50.

As we proceed in our study, we need to understand what this "great red dragon" represents (Revelation 12).

- The "great red dragon" is none other than Satan.
- The seven heads are seven kingdoms and their kings.
- The ten horns are ten nations the dragon will control.
- The seven diadems are crowns of the kings of seven nations.

POINTS TO PONDER

1. How did God's struggle with Satan begin?
2. Why did Satan rebel against God?
3. Was Satan behind the activities of Noah's day and the people of Sodom and Gomorrah?
4. If yes, how?

5

A Nation is Born

God used the events in Jacob's family to bring them into Egypt, where He would prepare them to be His people.

Why did God send Jacob's family to Egypt? Egypt, steeped in idolatrous worship, had a god for nearly every imaginable thing. Jacob and his entire family, including Joseph and his family, numbered seventy when taking up residence in Egypt. Genesis 46:1–4 tells us God would be with them:

> *So Israel took his journey with all that he had and came to Beersheba, and offered sacrifices to the God of his father Isaac. And God spoke to Israel in visions of the night and said, "Jacob, Jacob." And he said, "Here I am." Then he said, "I am God, the God of your father. Do not be afraid to go down to Egypt, for there I will make you into a great nation. I myself will go down with you to Egypt, and I will also bring you up again, and Joseph's hand shall close your eyes."*

God also revealed to Abraham how long they would be in this land.

> *As the sun was going down, a deep sleep fell on Abram. And behold, dreadful and great darkness fell upon him. Then the LORD said to Abram, "Know for certain that your offspring will be sojourners in a land that is not theirs and will be servants there, and they will be afflicted for four hundred years. But I will bring judgment on the nation that they serve, and afterward they shall come out with great possessions. As for you, you shall go to your fathers in peace; you shall be buried in a good old age. And they shall come back here in the fourth generation, for the iniquity of the Amorites is not yet complete."*
>
> **Genesis 15:12–16**

Israel in Egypt

When Jacob, his name changed to Israel, went down to Egypt during the famine, Joseph, who was sent to Egypt by divine appointment, told his brothers,

> *When Pharaoh calls you and says, "What is your occupation?" you shall say, "Your servants have been keepers of livestock from our youth even until now, both we and our fathers," in order that you may dwell in the land of Goshen, for every shepherd is an abomination to the Egyptians.*
>
> **Genesis 46:33–34**

> *However, when the brothers arrived in Egypt, they told the pharaoh when he asked, "'What is your occupation?' And they said to Pharaoh, 'Your servants are shepherds, as our fathers were'" (Genesis 47:3).*

Why did the brothers say they were shepherds when Joseph expressly told them to say otherwise? The answer, most likely, is that God needed to isolate the Israelites from the influence of Egyptian idolatry to keep them together, as He was preparing them to become a nation. This statement by Joseph's brothers likely prevented them from assimilating into Egyptian culture that would have exposed them to Egyptian idolatrous worship.

Israel finds itself dwelling in Egypt for 430 years (see Exodus 12:40). They arrived in Egypt around 1876 BCE with seventy family members, their number approaching two million at the time of the Exodus (see Exodus 12:37, Numbers 1:46 and 26:51). At some point following Joseph's death, the Israelites found themselves enslaved. Needing relief, they began to cry out to God for deliverance. God, hearing their cry, delivered them with a mighty hand through Moses, as recorded in the book of Exodus.

Egypt, founded around 3150 BCE by King Menes, flourished for a time with its ups and downs, during which it built the famous pyramids and the enslavement of the Israelite people. Israel escaped Egyptian bondage under the leadership of Moses, who was appointed by God for the task. The event, known as *the Exodus*, is recorded by

Moses in the second book of the Bible and is accepted to have occurred around 1446 BCE.

God sent a series of ten plagues, seemingly focusing on the idol deities of Egypt. Before the tenth plague, God gave Israel specific instructions to prepare them for the death of all the firstborn of Egypt, spared only by applying the blood as God instructed; failure to do so would bring death to the firstborn of the house (Exodus, chapters 7–12).

Following the tenth plague, all the firstborns of Egypt, not having the blood applied, died. The pharaoh initially allowed the Israelites to leave, but then hatred took over, and he pursued them with the intention of destroying them. God then performed the greatest miracle by parting the Red Sea, allowing the Israelites to escape the Egyptians. Once the Israelites passed over, the Red Sea returned to destroy the pharaoh's pursuing army. Satan's effort to destroy Israel failed, as God's hand of protection was upon them.

Egypt's power was broken by the Exodus event, even though it would survive until Alexander the Great defeated it in 332 BCE. Egypt's power remains until this day but under a different political system. Egypt is the *first* piece of the puzzle that we apply to the beast system of the end-time.

Egypt is the first head of the "great red dragon, with seven heads and ten horns, and on his head seven diadems" (Revelation 12:3).

A Nation is Born

Point to Ponder

How did the Hebrews (Jews) become a nation?

6
Israel and the Assyrians

After Israel departed Egypt, they went into the wilderness of Sinai and wandered there for forty years.

Israel entered the promised land around 1406 BCE and had great success if they followed God's commands. Eventually, they wandered away from God into idolatrous worship, which would lead to their defeat. Following Solomon's reign, the nation would divide. The tribes of Judah and Benjamin would remain using Jerusalem as their capital and be called *Judah*. The ten remaining northern tribes would secede from Judah and Benjamin and be called *Israel*, with Samaria as their capital. Israel's departure from worshiping God would ultimately lead to their destruction. Judah would soon follow.

Assyrian history dates back to about 1900 BCE, when their early kings seemed to be satisfied with trading merchandise with other peoples. From around 1804 to 1782 BCE, a king named Shamshi-Adad I expanded his territory. The Assyrians appeared to lapse into obscurity for a while but afterward became a major empire with which the Israelites had to deal.

The height of Assyrian power was from about 934 BCE to 609 BCE, when it fell. The Assyrian king Shalmaneser V reigned in 726–722 BCE. Assyria's intent toward the nations of Israel and Judah would be their destruction. God allowed them with their evil intentions to attack Israel and Judah but set limits as to how far their destruction would go. Israel was sieged and defeated.

The deportment of Israel and its resettlement with foreigners is attributed to Sargon, who reigned from 722–705 BCE, following the death of Shalmaneser V.

> *Ah, Assyria, the rod of my anger; the staff in their hands is my fury! Against a godless nation I send him, and against the people of my wrath I command him, to take spoil and seize plunder, and to tread them down like the mire of the streets. But he does not so intend, and his heart does not so think; but it is in his heart to destroy, and to cut off nations not a few.*
>
> **Isaiah 10:5–7**

God would allow Assyria to defeat the ten tribes of the northern kingdom known as Israel. However, when they attacked the southern kingdom of Judah, God limited them as to how far they could go (see 2 Kings 18:13–37; 19:1–37).

It was through the Assyrians that the ten tribes of Israel were dispersed to other lands. These tribes are now called the ten "lost tribes of Israel." We do not know where they are, but God does. "When the Lord has finished all his

Israel and the Assyrians

work on Mount Zion and on Jerusalem, he will punish the speech of the arrogant heart of the king of Assyria and the boastful look in his eyes" (Isaiah 10:12).

The Assyrian Empire is the second piece of the puzzle we apply to the beast system of the end-time.

Assyria is the *second* head of the "great red dragon, with seven heads and ten horns, and on his head seven diadems."

Points to Ponder

1. Why did God allow Assyria to war against Israel?
2. What happened to Israel?

7
Judah and the Babylonians

Judah seemed to be following in the footsteps of Israel. God used Jeremiah, a prophet, to warn them of their unfaithfulness to Him. Jeremiah begged them to repent, but they would not listen. He preached this message to them continuously, halfway through the reign of King Josiah and through the reigns of Jehoahaz, Jehoiakim, Jehoiachin, and through the end of the eleventh year of Zedekiah, king of Judah, when the people were exiled to Babylon.

Jeremiah warned them that if they did not repent, God would send them into exile for a period of seventy years.

Daniel was one of many who were deported to Babylon. He was a brilliant young man with a God-fearing character that was recognized by the ruling class of the Babylonians. It was there that God began using him as a prophet.

As the Assyrian Empire was in decline, a new powerful empire was emerging under the leadership of Nabopolassar.

He would be successful in ending the Assyrian Empire by destroying Nineveh in 612 BCE. Nebuchadnezzar ascended to power after his father's death in 605 BCE and created the largest ever Babylonian empire, ruling from Egypt to present-day Iran.

Nebuchadnezzar would attack Jerusalem several times in his efforts to enlarge his kingdom and bring Judah into subjection. Jehoiakim, king of Judah, would pay tribute to Babylon for several years, but in 601 BCE, he refused to pay. He then attacked Jerusalem which resulted in Jehoiakim's death. From this point on until 586 BCE, Nebuchadnezzar had to deal with the rebellious nation of Judah, appointing Jehoiakim's son, Jehoiachin, and Zedekiah to rule Judah as a vassal state of Babylon. During this period, Nebuchadnezzar attacked Jerusalem, carrying off temple treasures and ultimately destroying both the city and the temple. He also deported able-bodied residents of Jerusalem and Judah to Babylon and his empire. Daniel, Ezekiel, Haggai, and Zechariah were among those deported. Nebuchadnezzar promoted Daniel to a high position. Judah would serve Babylon in exile until the fulfillment of the seventy-year prophecy of Jeremiah 25:12:

> *Then after seventy years are completed, I will punish the king of Babylon and that nation, the land of the Chaldeans, for their iniquity, declares the LORD, making the land an everlasting waste.*

It was in Babylon that God would reveal the identity of the third, fourth, and fifth kingdoms that would appear on the earth.

Nebuchadnezzar Has a Dream

It all started when Nebuchadnezzar had a dream and asked his magicians and astrologers to tell him what his dream was and what it meant. See Daniel 2. They told the king there was not a man on the earth who could do what the king demanded. Daniel agreed with them but told the king there was a God in heaven who could reveal it. Daniel prayed, asking God to reveal the dream, which He did. Daniel then proceeded to reveal the dream God had given the king. The dream was about a large statue with a head of gold, arms and breast of silver, belly and thighs of brass, and legs of iron with feet a mixture of iron and clay. Daniel then interpreted the dream for the king as to what it meant:

> *You saw, O king, and behold, a great image. This image, mighty and of exceeding brightness, stood before you, and its appearance was frightening. The head of this image was of fine gold, its chest and arms of silver, its middle and thighs of bronze, its legs of iron, its feet partly of iron and partly of clay. As you looked, a stone was cut out by no human hand, and it struck the image on its feet of iron and clay, and broke them in pieces. Then the iron, the clay, the bronze, the silver, and the gold, all together were*

broken in pieces, and became like the chaff of the summer threshing floors; and the wind carried them away, so that not a trace of them could be found. But the stone that struck the image became a great mountain and filled the whole Earth. This was the dream. Now we will tell the king its interpretation. You, O king, the king of kings, to whom the God of heaven has given the kingdom, the power, and the might, and the glory, and into whose hand he has given, wherever they dwell, the children of man, the beasts of the field, and the birds of the heavens, making you rule over them all—you are the head of gold. Another kingdom inferior to you shall arise after you, and yet a third kingdom of bronze, which shall rule over all the Earth. And there shall be a fourth kingdom, strong as iron, because iron breaks to pieces and shatters all things. And like iron that crushes, it shall break and crush all these. And as you saw the feet and toes, partly of potter's clay and partly of iron, it shall be a divided kingdom, but some of the firmness of iron shall be in it, just as you saw iron mixed with the soft clay. And as the toes of the feet were partly iron and partly clay, so the kingdom shall be partly strong and partly brittle. As you saw the iron mixed with soft clay, so they will mix with one another in marriage, but they will not hold together, just as iron does not mix with clay. And in the days of those kings the God of heaven will set up a kingdom that shall never be destroyed, nor shall the kingdom be left to another people. It shall break in pieces all these kingdoms and bring them to an end, and it shall stand forever, just as you saw that a stone was cut from a mountain by no human hand, and that it broke in pieces the iron, the bronze, the clay, the silver, and the gold. A great God has made known to the king what shall be after this. The dream is certain, and its interpretation sure.

Daniel 2:31–45

God, through Daniel, tells us there will be four kingdoms appearing on the earth. He identified Babylonia as the *first kingdom* when he said to Nebuchadnezzar, "You are the head of gold" (verse 38). He then reveals three future kingdoms to follow that would bring about the establishment of God's kingdom.

He only identifies the second kingdom as the "arms and chest of silver" and the third kingdom as the "middle and thighs of brass" (verse 32). The fourth kingdom is identified as "its legs of iron, its feet partly of iron and partly of clay" (verse 33).

There is not much information about the second and third kingdoms, but the fourth kingdom will be

- "strong as iron" (verse 40),
- a divided kingdom (verse 41),
- partly strong and partly brittle (verse 42);
- it will not hold together (verse 43).

It appears this fourth kingdom will have strong "as iron" legs and eventually evolve into a divided kingdom with feet and toes of iron mixed with clay.

In the days of this fourth kingdom, God will establish His kingdom that will last forever.

Belshazzar would become king of Babylon following his father's death in 562 BCE. It was during Belshazzar's reign that Daniel received a vision from God.

Please read Daniel, chapter 7, before continuing.

The angel gives Daniel additional information concerning the same four kingdoms of Nebuchadnezzar's dream. He now identifies these four kingdoms as "beast" kingdoms (verse 3). He identifies them as different from one another. We already know the Babylonian kingdom was the first and identified as the "head of gold." The angel reveals to Daniel this kingdom was also like a lion and had eagle's wings (verse 4). We now understand a little more of the makeup of this first beast kingdom.

The first beast kingdom, revealed as the Babylonian kingdom, is motivated by wealth (gold) and conquering other nations by its aggressiveness and speed (lion with eagle's wings).

The second beast kingdom is now identified by the angel as a bear. No kingdom identification was given, only that it is told to devour much flesh. This beast kingdom represents the second kingdom of Nebuchadnezzar's dream, "the breast and arms of silver" (Daniel 2:32).

Judah and the Babylonians

We can now ascertain the makeup of this second beast kingdom as having wealth represented by silver and the disposition and aggressiveness of a bear.

Again, no identification of the third beast kingdom was given, but we can recognize its wealth as brass and its disposition as that of a leopard.

The fourth beast kingdom is also not identified, only that it will be the last kingdom to arise before God sets up His eternal kingdom.

At this point in our understanding of the fourth beast kingdom, we see that Nebuchadnezzar's dream identifies it as a kingdom of iron and clay and that it will be a "divided" kingdom. Now the angel gives Daniel some added characteristics of this fourth kingdom:

- It will be "terrifying and dreadful and exceedingly strong" (Daniel 7:7).
- "It had great iron teeth" (Daniel 7:7).
- It *was different*. Little or no wealth seems to be associated with it, so the kingdom has other ambitions (Daniel 7:7, 23).
- Its makeup was "iron and clay" (militarily strong but politically weak), a divided kingdom (Daniel 2:41).

Following this kingdom, God would set up His own that would rule forever. Daniel then receives another vision that sheds even more light on the makeup of these kingdoms.

God's End-Time Puzzle

Please read Daniel, chapter 8, before continuing.

Daniel, in Nebuchadnezzar's vision, was given the identity and understanding of the head of gold as the *Babylonian kingdom* of which Nebuchadnezzar was the king. Now, the angel is giving identity to the second kingdom as the *Medo-Persian kingdom*, the two-horned ram, and the third beast kingdom, the shaggy goat, is identified as the *Grecian kingdom*. These first two kingdoms of Daniel's chapter 8 vision have been shown by the angel to represent the second and third kingdoms of Nebuchadnezzar's statue. Daniel, in his visions of chapters 7 and 8, has much to say concerning this last, or fourth, beast kingdom appearing on the earth. Bible historians seem to equate this fourth kingdom to the *Roman kingdom*. Up to this point, the identification of the first three cannot be challenged, as the Bible has explicitly identified them. However, no identity has been given to this last, or fourth, kingdom that shall appear. The identity of this last kingdom as being the *revived Roman kingdom* is extremely questionable, as it does not appear until the end.

Daniel's description of the second beast kingdom as being the Medo-Persian kingdom (verse 20), followed by the third beast kingdom from Greece (verse 21), is proven true. Nearly all Bible scholars agree these are successive kingdoms. The Babylonian kingdom was defeated by Cyrus, the primary king of the Medo-Persian kingdom, in 539 BCE, who allowed the Jews to return to their homeland.

Judah and the Babylonians

- The Scriptures identify the last of these four as appearing at the end of time.
- The Roman Empire does not match the description of this last kingdom.
- The Western Roman Empire ceased to exist in 476 CE, never having met the criteria laid out by Daniel's visions. The same can be said for the Eastern portion of the Roman Empire, which lasted until 1453 CE.

Daniel has given us information that the Babylonian Empire is, in fact, the *third* piece of the puzzle that we apply to the beast system of the end-time.

When Daniel was given further clarity on his vision in chapter 8, it was revealed to him that the king of the Grecian kingdom would die and that his Grecian kingdom would be divided among his four generals. It was then disclosed to Daniel that "out of one of them" (we will explore this in a later chapter) would arise a king who would be the ruler of the last beast kingdom on the earth that would be destroyed by the King of kings and Lord of lords. This last kingdom would come out of one of the kingdoms of the four generals of Alexander the Great's Grecian kingdom.

The Babylonian kingdom is the third head but the *first beast* of the "great red dragon, with seven heads and ten horns, and on his head seven diadems."

Points to Ponder
1. Why did Nebuchadnezzar have a dream?
2. What was Daniel's role concerning the dream?
3. What did the dream reveal?
4. Why did Daniel have visions?
5. What did his visions reveal?

8

Israel and the Medo-Persian Empire

Isaiah the prophet declared around 712 BCE that a king by the name of Cyrus would make a proclamation to rebuild the city and temple in Jerusalem: "Who says of Cyrus, 'He is my shepherd, and he shall fulfill all my purpose'; saying of Jerusalem, 'She shall be built,' and of the temple, 'Your foundation shall be laid'" (Isaiah 44:28).

Now, almost 160 years later, an empire called the Medo-Persian Empire defeats the Babylonian Empire. The king is none other than Cyrus, the one prophesied by Isaiah.

One of the first things Cyrus does is to allow the Jews who wanted to go back and rebuild the temple in Jerusalem to do so, just as Isaiah prophesied.

> *In the first year of Cyrus king of Persia, that the word of the* Lord *by the mouth of*

> *Jeremiah might be fulfilled, the LORD stirred up the spirit of Cyrus king of Persia, so that he made a proclamation throughout all his Kingdom and also put it in writing: "Thus says Cyrus king of Persia: The LORD, the God of heaven, has given me all the Kingdoms of the Earth, and he has charged me to build him a house at Jerusalem, which is in Judah. Whoever is among you of all his people, may his God be with him, and let him go up to Jerusalem, which is in Judah, and rebuild the house of the LORD, the God of Israel—he is the God who is in Jerusalem.*
>
> **Ezra 1:1–3**

Jeremiah also prophesied that Israel would be exiled for seventy years, after which the Babylonian Empire would be destroyed.

> *Therefore thus says the LORD of hosts: Because you have not obeyed my words, behold, I will send for all the tribes of the north, declares the LORD, and for Nebuchadnezzar, the king of Babylon, my servant, and I will bring them against this land and its inhabitants, and against all these surrounding nations. I will devote them to destruction, and make them a horror, a hissing, and an everlasting desolation. Moreover, I will banish from them the voice of mirth and the voice of gladness, the voice of the bridegroom and the voice of the bride, the grinding of the millstones and the light of the lamp. This whole land shall*

become a ruin and waste, and these nations shall serve the king of Babylon seventy years. Then after seventy years are completed, I will punish the king of Babylon and that nation, the land of the Chaldeans, for their iniquity, declares the LORD, *making the land an everlasting waste.*

Jeremiah 25:8–12

Thus, Jeremiah's and Isaiah's prophecies were fulfilled at the same time.

At some point early in the reign of the Medo-Persian Empire, Daniel had already experienced the first "beast empire," the Babylonian Empire, and the arrival around 538 BCE of the second "beast empire," the Medo-Persian Empire, with a seemingly benevolent attitude toward the Jews. Many Jews would accept the offer of Cyrus for them to return to the holy land. Most would not. After all, they were scattered throughout the Babylonian Empire. Living there for seventy years, they had established roots, raised families, and were relatively comfortable in their situation.

Cyrus, defeating the Babylonian Empire, seemed to bring hope to the Jews. His generosity in allowing many to return to Jerusalem seemed to revive their spirits. However, in due time, this second "beast empire" would raise its ugly head.

Jerusalem remained under the rule of the Medo-Persian Empire, even though Cyrus had allowed the Jews to return to Jerusalem to rebuild the temple. Residents of the area would oppose their rebuilding efforts. Also, the book of Esther would reveal a demonic plan to exterminate all Jews remaining throughout the entire Medo-Persian Empire. The plan, however, was found out and foiled. Even though God is not mentioned in the book of Esther, it is evident God was looking out for His people. This event occurred under King Xerxes I, who ruled the Medo-Persian Empire from 486 to 465 BCE.

It was early during this Medo-Persian Empire rule that Daniel again received a vision from God. The vision appeared while Daniel was praying for the forgiveness of his people. This vision, as recorded in Daniel 9, does not deal with the arrival of the beast empires as in previous ones. It deals with a very important fact—the future of the Jewish nation. We will not delve into the specifics of this history at this point, as we are dealing with the beast kingdoms arriving on the earth, culminating in the battle of Armageddon.

The Medo-Persian Empire remained in control of Judah and the holy land until Alexander the Great defeated and assumed control of the Grecian Empire. He was only nineteen years old when he began to reign. In 334 BCE, he began a campaign to conquer the Medo-Persian Empire, eventually conquering Babylon, their seat of authority, in 331 BCE, another piece of the puzzle.

The Medo-Persian Empire is the fourth head but the *second beast* of the "great red dragon, with seven heads and ten horns, and on his head seven diadems."

Israel and the Medo-Persian Empire

Points to Ponder

1. Who was the king of the Medo-Persian Empire?
2. What did Isaiah have to say about him?
3. What was one of the first things he did?

refers to the appointed time of the end. As for the ram that you saw with the two horns, these are the kings of Media and Persia. And the goat is the king of Greece. And the great horn between his eyes is the first king. As for the horn that was broken, in place of which four others arose, four Kingdoms shall arise from his nation, but not with his power. And at the latter end of their Kingdom, when the transgressors have reached their limit, a king of bold face, one who understands riddles, shall arise. His power shall be great—but not by his own power; and he shall cause fearful destruction and shall succeed in what he does, and destroy mighty men and the people who are the saints. By his cunning he shall make deceit prosper under his hand, and in his own mind he shall become great. Without warning he shall destroy many. And he shall even rise up against the Prince of princes, and he shall be broken—but by no human hand. The vision of the evenings and the mornings that has been told is true, but seal up the vision, for it refers to many days from now."

Daniel 8:15–26

There is one important element in the vision given to Daniel that was not in the explanation Gabriel gave to Daniel. It was a fact that was in the vision recorded in Daniel 8:8–11:

Israel and the Grecian Empire

Then the goat became exceedingly great, but when he was strong, the great horn was broken, and instead of it there came up four conspicuous horns toward the four winds of heaven. Out of one of them came a little horn, which grew exceedingly great toward the south, toward the east, and toward the glorious land. It grew great, even to the host of heaven. And some of the host and some of the stars it threw down to the ground and trampled on them. It became great, even as great as the Prince of the host. And the regular burnt offering was taken away from him, and the place of his sanctuary was overthrown.

"Out of one of them" (verse 9) refers to one of the four divisions of the Grecian Empire. Gabriel is revealing to us that the Antichrist will emerge from out of one of these four divisions.

Following the fall of the Medo-Persian Empire, Alexander the Great would become ill and die at the age of thirty-two. His kingdom was divided among four of his generals, as revealed in this vision given to Daniel over 150 years before Alexander the Great marched into Babylon, defeating the once-mighty Medo-Persian Empire. The vision was accurate, as Alexander's kingdom was divided into four kingdoms following his death.

These four kingdoms are still considered to be Grecian. The divisions are Ptolemaic, Antigonid, Hellenistic, and Seleucid. The eastern division was ruled by Seleucus over an area of modern-day Afghanistan, Iran, Iraq, Syria, and Lebanon, together with parts of Turkey, Armenia, Turkmenistan, Uzbekistan, and Tajikistan. This division was where Antiochus IV Epiphanes would eventually rule. He was the ruler who invaded Jerusalem and caused an *abomination of desolation* of the temple by sacrificing a pig on the altar. It was this division that Daniel referred to when he said in verse 9, "Out of one of them came a little horn." It is out of this kingdom, the northern division of the Grecian Empire, that I believe the Antichrist will emerge. It is this kingdom, not the Roman Empire, that will produce the ten-nation confederacy of the end-time.

In the third year of Cyrus, king of the Medo-Persian Empire, Daniel receives a vision concerning the events between the king of the south (the Ptolemaic Kingdom) and the king of the north (the Seleucid Kingdom). These events occurred from the time of the Grecian Empire's division in 323 BCE to when Antiochus Epiphanes set up an *abomination causing desolation* on the twenty-fifth day of December in 167 BCE by sacrificing a pig in God's temple. Daniel predicted these events some 350 years before they happened.

These events, however, are *only shadows of end-time events*. Jesus refers to Daniel's prophecy in Matthew 24:15, "So, when you see the *abomination of desolation* spoken of by the prophet Daniel, standing in the holy place (let the reader understand)."

This abomination referred to by Jesus will occur in the middle of the last week of Daniel's seventy-week prophecy.

Israel and the Grecian Empire

> *And he shall make a strong covenant with many for one week, and for half of the week he shall put an end to sacrifice and offering. And on the wing of abominations shall come one who makes desolate, until the decreed end is poured out on the desolator.*
>
> **Daniel 9:27**

Three of the four beast kingdoms identified by Daniel have already existed and perished from the earth, leaving only the fourth beast kingdom (yet unknown) with which to deal. However, as we begin to explore this fourth beast kingdom, we see it has a close relationship to the third beast kingdom. In discovering the details of this fourth kingdom, we can see a gap of time between the third and fourth kingdoms. A gap that is seen by the scholars but has its beginning point at the wrong time. It seems they place this gap between the ending of the Roman Empire and the rise of what they call the "revived Roman Empire." The evidence will show the gap begins at the end of the Grecian Empire. It is here that the narrative switches from the third beast empire to the fourth beast empire. To discover the truth of this, we must again look at Daniel's vision concerning this last empire to appear on the earth. The Grecian Empire is an important piece of the end-time puzzle.

The Grecian Empire is the fifth head but the *third beast* of the "great red dragon, with seven heads and ten horns, and on his head seven diadems."

Points to Ponder
1. Who was the king of the Grecian Empire?
2. What happened to his kingdom?
3. How does it fit in the future?

10

Israel and the Roman Empire

It is at this point that we can seemingly all agree that the events of the kingdoms up through the Grecian Empire are accurate. However, when Daniel's vision ended with the Grecian Empire and turned to the last (eighth) empire of the Antichrist, the understanding went in several directions.

- The most prevalent view (especially in the Western world) seems to believe that the Roman Empire will be revived and bring forth the eighth empire of the Antichrist.
- Germany is also mentioned as a candidate.
- The Holy Roman Empire is a possibility.
- Also, Islam is believed to be involved.

From this point forward, I am going to set forth the reasons I believe, my understanding, of what occurs and brings us to the kingdom of the Antichrist and his activities until he is defeated at the battle of Armageddon.

No one has proof that their opinions and understandings are true, including me. We all must wait and follow what is politically going on in the world. Time will reveal who is right.

The visions given to Daniel concerning the beast kingdoms rising on the earth have all come and gone except the fourth beast kingdom, which needs revealing. John will reveal the Roman Empire is the sixth in the line of empires rising against the Jewish people. Following will be a seventh "not yet come" empire before the *fourth beast empire* emerges.

It is at this point that we can seemingly all agree that the events up through the Grecian Empire are accurate. However, when Daniel's vision ended with the Grecian Empire, it turned his attention to the last empire of the Antichrist. The understanding of how the empires following the Grecian Empire play out remains to be seen.

The most prevalent view, especially in the Western world, seems to believe that the Roman Empire will be revived to bring forth the empire of the Antichrist; others disagree. We will explore this as we continue in our study.

The Roman Empire, responsible for defeating the Grecian Seleucid division in 63 BCE, took over the rule of Judea, the home of the Jews. There seems to be no indication of any of the "beast" visions given to Daniel that would even hint at Roman involvement as the fourth beast kingdom. All his visions concerning this fourth beast kingdom are placed at the end of the age. Most scholars seem to believe the Roman Empire is the empire that will be revived to bring about the beast kingdom of the end-time.

Some scholars want to equate the vision Daniel received in Daniel 9:24–27 with the destruction of the city and sanctuary by Titus in 70 CE, but is it? Let us look very closely at what Daniel said about his vision.

> *Seventy weeks are decreed about your people and your holy city, to finish the transgression, to put an end to sin, and to atone for iniquity, to bring in everlasting righteousness, to seal both vision and prophet, and to anoint a most holy place. Know therefore and understand that from the going out of the word to restore and build Jerusalem to the coming of an anointed one, a prince, there shall be seven weeks. Then for sixty-two weeks it shall be built again with squares and moat, but in a troubled time. And after the sixty-two weeks, an anointed one shall be cut off and shall have nothing. And the people of the prince who is to come shall destroy the city and the sanctuary. Its end shall come with a flood, and to the end there shall be war. Desolations are decreed. And he shall make a strong covenant with many for one week, and for half of the week he shall put an end to sacrifice and offering. And on the wing of abominations shall come one who makes desolate, until the decreed end is poured out on the desolator.*
>
> **Daniel 9:24–27**

God's End-Time Puzzle

The proper understanding of this vision tells us that during the sixty-two weeks, the temple and city would be rebuilt. Following this sixty-two-week period, the anointed one, the Messiah, would be "cut off" (crucified). Did this happen? The answer is a resounding *yes*.

Daniel, in his prophecy, has revealed to us that God is giving Israel a period of 490 years to fulfill the requirements He has set forth for them to accomplish.

- "Finish the transgression." Put an end to their rebellion that will occur when Jesus returns to set up His kingdom.
- "Put an end to sin." When Satan has been defeated and imprisoned, there will be no more sin for 1,000 years.
- "Atone for iniquity." It was fulfilled when Christ shed His blood for the atonement of our sins.
- "Bring in everlasting righteousness." Again, this will occur when Jesus returns.
- "To seal both vision and prophet." The prophecy was sealed to be opened and understood at the appropriate time.
- "And to anoint a most holy place." The KJV and NIV versions say "to anoint the most Holy," and it is generally thought to mean when Jesus is anointed as the Prophet, Priest, and King.

Most scholars believe that the seventy-week period began when Artaxerxes gave a decree to Nehemiah to rebuild Jerusalem in 445 BCE.

Israel and the Roman Empire

The context of verses 26 and 27 above shows "the people of the prince who is to come shall destroy the city and the sanctuary" is a reference to the end-time, as "he" of verse 27 is a reference to the "prince of the people." Also, it is this prince, I believe, who makes the covenant that begins the seventieth week of Daniel's prophecy. The prince is none other than the Antichrist.

John tells us in Revelation 17:7–8,

> *But the angel said to me, "Why do you marvel? I will tell you the mystery of the woman, and of the beast with seven heads and ten horns that carries her. The beast that you saw was, and is not, and is about to rise from the bottomless pit and go to destruction. And the dwellers on Earth whose names have not been written in the book of life from the foundation of the world will marvel to see the beast, because it was and is not and is to come."*

Note: the angel says, "[...] was and is not." This beast could not be the Roman Empire because it was then in existence, which rules it out. The division of the old Grecian Empire, on the other hand, had existed previously but had ceased to exist in 63 BCE. At the time of John's writing, the old Grecian Empire did not exist. The conclusion must be that one of the divisions of the Grecian Empire is the beast of the end-time that will "rise from the bottomless pit." Daniel has stated in 8:9, "out of one of them," referring to the four divisions of the Grecian kingdom as where this beast will come from—not from the Roman Empire.

The misunderstanding of this truth originates in Daniel's prophecy of the seventy weeks.

The text of Daniel 9:26 was understood to have occurred at the time when the city and the temple were destroyed in 70 CE by Titus, with the scripture that is following referring to the end-time. Confusion could occur because it would place the Romans as "the people of the prince who is to come." If we take the evidence the Romans were not in view, according to John's prophecy, then we would have to understand that "the people of the prince who is to come" refers only to the end-time. The ruler, then, who will come is the Antichrist, which places the people of the end-time as the ones who will destroy the city and the sanctuary. Who else can it be? The question is: Who are "the people of the prince who is to come"? We will deal with this in a later chapter.

The Roman Empire is to be treated just like the Egyptian and Assyrian empires in their relationship to the "great red dragon." This piece of the puzzle must be placed in the makeup of the beast system of the end-time, but we must be careful where we place it.

The Roman Empire is the *sixth* head of the "great red dragon, with seven heads and ten horns, and on his head seven diadems."

Points to Ponder

1. What does Daniel reveal about the Roman Empire?
2. What important prophecy was partially fulfilled in the Roman Empire's day?

BEFORE CONTINUING

Let us first look at some of these empires. Daniel revealed the identity of three of them. The first three, according to Daniel, were the Babylonian, Medo-Persian, and Grecian empires. John, in Revelation 17:9–10, tells us:

> *This calls for a mind with wisdom: the seven heads are seven mountains on which the woman is seated; they are also seven kings, five of whom have fallen, one is, the other has not yet come, and when he does come he must remain only a little while.*

We can now understand that "one is" refers to the Roman Empire of John's day. That places the Roman Empire as the sixth in the list of the seven empires that arise on the earth.

Working from this information, we can determine the list as follows:

1.	The Egyptian Empire	
2.	The Assyrian Empire	
3.	The Babylonian Empire*	five fallen empires
4.	The Medo-Persian Empire*	
5.	The Grecian Empire*	
6.	The Roman Empire	one that is
7.	The Ottoman Empire	
8.	The empire of the beast, the Antichrist*	"not yet come"

*The four beasts that are referred to by the angel in Daniel 7:17.

Daniel further identifies these beast empires:

- The first *beast* was the Babylonian Empire and was like *a lion and had eagle's wings* (Daniel 7:4).
- The second *beast* was the Medo-Persian Empire; it was like a *bear* and was told to devour much flesh (Daniel 7:5).
- The third *beast* was the Grecian Empire with the disposition of a *leopard* (Daniel 7:6).
- The fourth *beast*, the end-time beast, will have all the characteristics of these three previous beast empires.

> *And the beast that I saw was like a leopard; its feet were like a bear's, and its mouth was like a lion's mouth. And to it the dragon gave his power and his throne and great authority.*
> **Revelation 13:2**

We will explore this more fully in a later chapter.

11

The "Not Yet Come" Empire

As we have noted in Daniel's visions of the beast empires, they jump from the third beast, the Grecian Empire, to the fourth beast empire without ever mentioning the Roman Empire. The fourth beast empire is the empire of the Antichrist, which Jesus will defeat at the battle of Armageddon. John also reveals to us that following the Roman Empire, a seventh empire will arise before the eighth empire of the Antichrist.

> *They are also seven kings, five of whom have fallen, one is, the other has not yet come, and when he does come he must remain only a little while. As for the beast that was and is not, it is an eighth but it belongs to the seven, and it goes to destruction.*
> **Revelation 17:10–11**

What is this "not yet come" empire of verse 10 above? Most end-time writers and preachers claim that the legs and feet of Nebuchadnezzar's statue represent the Roman Empire that fell in 1453 CE. They then say it is the revived Roman Empire bringing about the empire of the Antichrist. I believe this is wrong. All empires, from the Egyptian to the Roman, have come and gone. All were enemies of God's people. However, not all were designated as "beast empires."

The Egyptians were defeated by the Assyrians, who were defeated by the Babylonians, who were defeated by the Medo-Persians, who were defeated by the Grecians, who were defeated by the Romans. The Ottoman Empire defeated the Romans in 1453 CE, but end-time writers and preachers want us to ignore this and believe it will be a revived Roman Empire bringing about the empire of the Antichrist. However, the scripture above says, "one is," referring to the Roman Empire existing at the time. Next, it says, "the other has not yet come." How can the Roman Empire be the one that "is" and still be the one that is "not yet come"? Do they want you to believe that the one that "is" has really "not yet come"? What the scripture is really telling us is that the Roman Empire "is" (i.e., existed at that time) and that there is another empire "yet to come."

Are we then to understand the Roman Empire will be defeated with no existence for over 600+ years and then be revived to produce the "beast empire" of the Antichrist?

I believe it makes no sense to accept this understanding. The pattern of the past empires is an empire rises in power to defeat a previous empire. This pattern holds throughout all the empires of the past.

The "Not Yet Come" Empire

The Roman Empire is no different. The eastern division of the Roman Empire was defeated by the Ottoman Empire when Sultan Mehmed II conquered Constantinople and renamed it Istanbul.

I believe the Ottoman Empire is the "not yet come" empire of Revelation 17:10.

The "great red dragon" is Satan; he has been building his "dragon" of opposition to God's people since the beginning; it is not reasonable to think he has taken a 600+ year vacation from his efforts.

The Ottoman Empire has been ruled by Islam founded by Muhammad throughout their history, its politics being governed by its religious beliefs. The two legs of Nebuchadnezzar's statue, I believe, represent the two factions of Islamic belief, the Sunnis and Shiites.

The Ottoman Empire, the seventh "not yet come" empire of John's prophecy, came to an end in 1922 CE. Daniel reveals to us that the empire of the Antichrist, the fourth "beast empire," will be different. How so? The Islamic political Ottoman Empire is gone, but the religious empire has survived, seemingly having great influence over many nations.

If my understanding is correct, this different kingdom, the Islamic kingdom proclaiming Allah as their God, is the seventh kingdom that will bring forth the Antichrist. This is the piece of the puzzle many have overlooked, but it is extremely important for us to see the right picture.

In looking at the makeup of this seven-headed dragon with ten horns, we see the seventh empire is the Islamic religious empire. The political faction is no more, but the religious faction has remained and is worldwide, headed by the Islamic god, Allah (Satan). We will discover that Satan will be cast down to the earth. When he is cast down, he will possess the Antichrist, who, most likely, has already established the eighth (fourth beast) kingdom of Daniel's prophecy.

The Ottoman Empire is the *seventh* head of the "great red dragon, with seven heads and ten horns, and on his head seven diadems."

Points to Ponder

1. What is the importance of the "not yet come" empire?
2. Who is the "not yet come" empire?
3. What follows this empire?

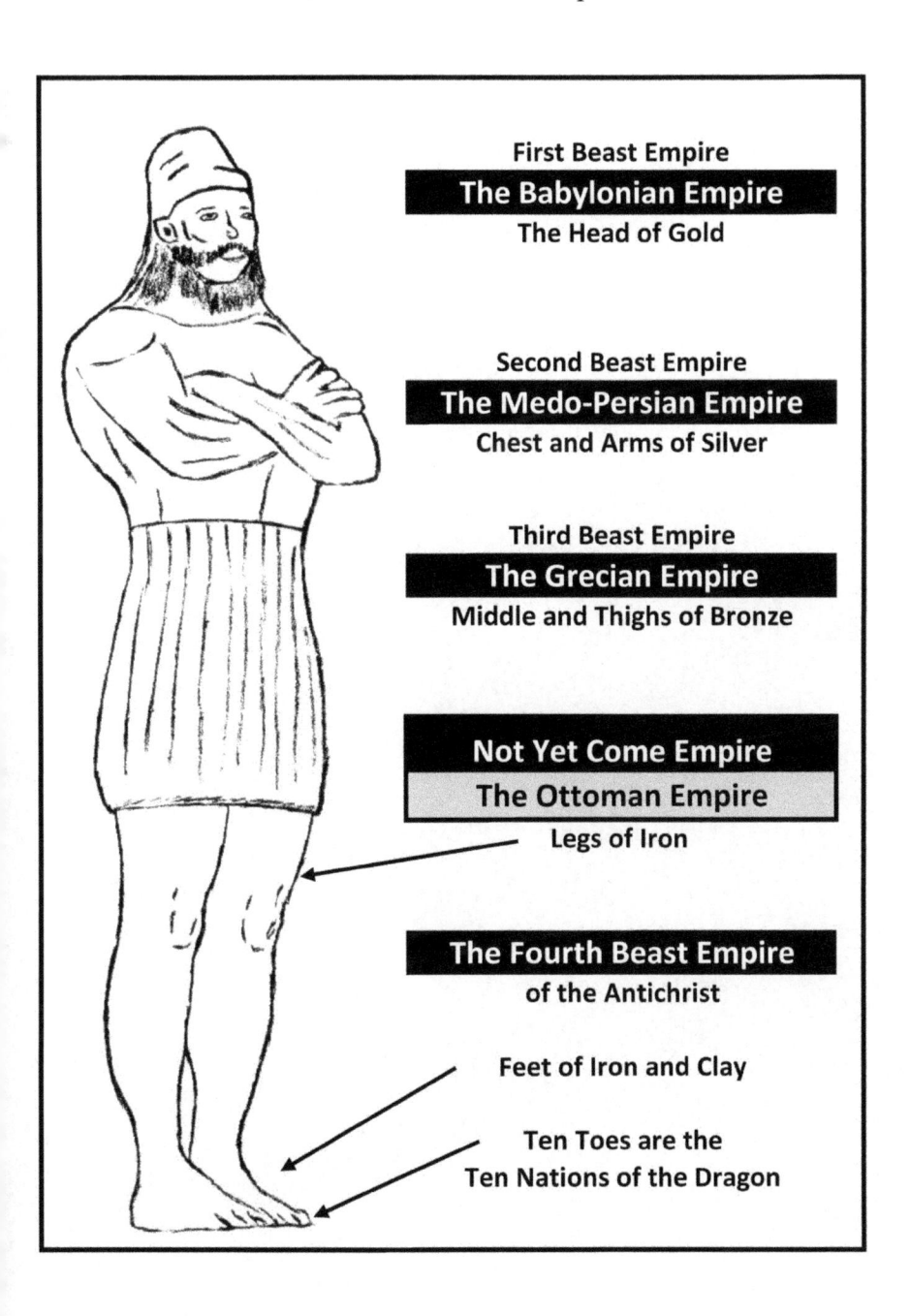

The "Not Yet Come" Empire

First Beast Empire
The Babylonian Empire
The Head of Gold

Second Beast Empire
The Medo-Persian Empire
Chest and Arms of Silver

Third Beast Empire
The Grecian Empire
Middle and Thighs of Bronze

Not Yet Come Empire
The Ottoman Empire
Legs of Iron

The Fourth Beast Empire
of the Antichrist

Feet of Iron and Clay

Ten Toes are the
Ten Nations of the Dragon

12

The Fourth Beast Empire

The first inkling we have as to when the appearance of this "fourth beast" will occur is found in Revelation 12:3: "And another sign appeared in heaven: behold, a great red dragon, with seven heads and ten horns, and on his heads seven diadems."

This scripture gives us information that Satan, the dragon, is the power and the force behind this fourth beast kingdom.

In Revelation 13:1–2, we see:

> *And I saw a beast rising out of the sea, with ten horns and seven heads, with ten diadems on its horns and blasphemous names on its heads. And the beast that I saw was like a leopard; its feet were like a bear's, and its mouth was like a lion's mouth. And to it the dragon gave his power and his throne and great authority.*

Four things emerge from this information concerning this fourth "beast" making its entrance during this time.

1. The "beast" is also the king of the fourth and last beast kingdom, and it has *ten horns, seven heads*, and *ten diadems*. The horns represent this fourth beast as a coalition of ten nations that have formed an alliance with political, economic, and spiritual powers. These ten nations, I believe, are already in existence. They are Islamic nations ruled by Sharia law. The Antichrist, when he comes, will be so charismatic that he will have no problem uniting these nations under his spiritual leadership. The "beast" (the coalition of nations) could emerge quite rapidly under the leadership of the Antichrist. The Antichrist and his coalition of nations will, I believe, be the ones who will make a seven-year covenant with Israel. Revelation 13:2 reveals that Satan empowers the "beast" (king or ruler) with "his power and his throne and great authority." When Satan was cast out of heaven, he came down to the earth and indwelt (possessed) the Antichrist. It is then Satan himself who will become the beast (ruler/king) of this eighth kingdom, which is the fourth beast kingdom.

2. We notice the dragon (Satan) only has seven heads (the seven previous nations), but this kingdom is the eighth (fourth beast kingdom) in the line of kingdoms rising on the earth. I believe that, since Satan is the dragon and he gives *all* his power unto the Antichrist and to his kingdom, he will embody all the characteristics of the three beast kingdoms preceding it. It will be the dragon (Satan) himself who rules this coalition of nations through the

The Fourth Beast Empire

Antichrist, becoming the fourth beast kingdom and the eighth in the list of kingdoms to arise on the earth. Also, Revelation 17:8 reveals this kingdom has already existed, so it is one of the previous kingdoms. The eighth, the kingdom of the Antichrist, is also the fourth beast kingdom.

3. What about the information that there are *seven heads* (kingdoms), *ten horns* (nations), and *seven diadems* (crowns)? To understand, we must look at John's vision in Revelation 17:7–10:

> *But the angel said to me, "Why do you marvel? I will tell you the mystery of the woman, and of the beast with seven heads and ten horns that carries her. The beast that you saw was, and is not, and is about to rise from the bottomless pit and go to destruction. And the dwellers on Earth whose names have not been written in the book of life from the foundation of the world will marvel to see the beast, because it was and is not and is to come. This calls for a mind with wisdom: the seven heads are seven mountains on which the woman is seated; they are also seven kings, five of whom have fallen, one is, the other has not yet come, and when he does come he must remain only a little while."*

Notice that *the seven heads are seven mountains* (kingdoms) and that *they are also seven kings*. These kings representing seven kingdoms seem to contradict what Daniel has to say concerning the beast kingdoms. To understand this, we must look at the kingdoms beginning with the Babylonian, followed by the Medo-Persian, and then by the Grecian. The last of these three, the Grecian kingdom, ceased to exist in 63 BCE. When John is given information concerning the witnesses that God sent to the earth to confront the activities of the Satan-possessed Antichrist, he reveals to us that the beast comes up out of the bottomless pit: "And when they have finished their testimony, the beast that *rises from the bottomless pit* will make war on them and conquer them and kill them" (Revelation 11:7).

    4.   The "beast" resembled three "beasts."

> *"And the beast that I saw was like a leopard; its feet were like a bear's, and its mouth was like a lion's mouth. And to it the dragon gave his power and his throne and great authority" (Revelation 13:2).*

This fourth beast will have all the attributes of the first three beast kingdoms of Daniel's prophecies. All the speed, evil, and hatred rolled up into one. The fourth beast kingdom is also the eighth kingdom. The dragon (Satan) gave this beast *all* his power and authority. It is Satan's last-ditch effort to defeat God and destroy His people.

Daniel, in his visions concerning these empires appearing on the earth, begins with Nebuchadnezzar's statue showing four kingdoms. Later, Daniel has a vision showing these same four kingdoms but with attributes not seen in the statue. Still, later he sees a vision showing only three empires: the Medo-Persian, the Grecian, and the

The Fourth Beast Empire

final kingdom. His visions did not include the Egyptian or the Assyrian empires. He tells us in Daniel 8:8–9,

> *Then the goat became exceedingly great, but when he was strong, the great horn was broken, and instead of it there came up four conspicuous horns toward the four winds of heaven. Out of one of them came a little horn, which grew exceedingly great toward the south, toward the east, and toward the glorious land.*

Daniel informs us that *out of one* of the four divisions of the Grecian Empire came another horn that develops a kingdom that grows in power, "To the south and to the east and toward the Beautiful Land" (Daniel 8:9, NIV). ("Beautiful Land" means the promised land, or Israel.) It seems obvious this kingdom comes out of the easternmost (Seleucid) division of the four divisions of the old Grecian Empire, as Daniel devotes the balance of this prophecy to it.

These prophecies have all been fulfilled and understood except the fourth kingdom. The third beast kingdom, the one we call the Grecian Kingdom, ceased to exist in 63 BCE. Daniel does not see the Roman Empire just as he did not see the Egyptian or Assyrian empires. What are we to make of that? God, through the visions recorded in Daniel, revealed only the information necessary for us to understand the order of events leading up to and including the end-time. The Roman Empire is shown in Jesus's revelation to John through the angels only for the purpose of continuity until this end-time kingdom should rise. The Western Roman Empire fell in about 476 CE after a gradual decline when the last emperor, Romulus Augustus, was dethroned. The Eastern Roman Empire lasted until Constantinople fell in about 1453 CE. At that point, it was the Ottoman Empire that became the "not yet come" empire, not the *revived Roman Empire*. The seventh empire of John's prophecy was a Muslim (Islamic) empire. The political ceased to be, but the spiritual remained—the divided empire referenced by Daniel 2:41.

Are we then to expect this seventh empire would appear on the scene at approximately the same time as the expiration of the Eastern Roman Empire? The answer is yes. Then what empire came into the picture, meeting Daniel's criteria of its makeup?

First, let's look at the Egyptian and the Assyrian empires. They had no apparent role in how this end-time empire would emerge. The evidence seems to show the Babylonian Empire would be overtaken by the Medo-Persian Empire, which would be overtaken by the Grecian Empire, whose emperor was Alexander the Great. When Alexander the Great died, his generals divided the empire into four territories. The eastern one was known as the Seleucid division. It was out of this division, according to what Daniel prophesied, that the Antichrist would come. He reveals to us a "shadow" of the eighth kingdom (fourth beast) to come (see Daniel, chapter 11). The Roman Empire was next in line, but there seems to be no information except what John mentions. It was after the fall of the Roman Empire that the seventh empire would appear. If this understanding is correct, then this seventh empire would appear from somewhere out of the land of the Seleucid division of the Grecian Empire. It is not the revived Roman Empire that appears, nor is it the revived Grecian Empire, for Daniel says this fourth beast empire will be *different* from the others. Let us look and seek an understanding of why this seventh empire is different.

Let us look at Nebuchadnezzar's dream of the statue and what God revealed to him through Daniel as to what this fourth beast would be.

> *And there shall be a fourth Kingdom, strong as iron, because iron breaks to pieces and shatters all things. And like iron that crushes, it shall break and crush all these. And as you saw the feet and toes, partly of potter's clay and partly of iron, it shall be a divided Kingdom, but some of the firmness of iron shall be in it, just as you saw iron mixed with the soft clay. And as the toes of the feet were partly iron and partly clay, so the Kingdom shall be partly strong and partly brittle. As you saw the iron mixed with soft clay, so they will mix with one another in marriage, but they will not hold together, just as iron does not mix with clay. And in the days of those kings the God of heaven will set up a Kingdom that shall never be destroyed, nor shall the Kingdom be left to another people. It shall break in pieces all these Kingdoms and bring them to an end, and it shall stand forever, just as you saw that a stone was cut*

> *from a mountain by no human hand, and that it broke in pieces the iron, the bronze, the clay, the silver, and the gold. A great God has made known to the king what shall be after this. The dream is certain, and its interpretation sure.*
>
> **Daniel 2:40–45**

From this point on, we must consider the Ottoman Empire as the seventh empire but not the beast empire of the end-time. The end-time "beast empire" is the ten-nation confederacy ruled by the Antichrist, the feet and toes of Nebuchadnezzar's statue. Next, let's look at Daniel 7:7–8:

> *After this I saw in the night visions, and behold, a fourth Beast, terrifying and dreadful and exceedingly strong. It had great iron teeth; it devoured and broke in pieces and stamped what was left with its feet. It was different from all the Beasts that were before it, and it had ten horns. I considered the horns, and behold, there came up among them another horn, a little one, before which three of the first horns were plucked up by the roots. And behold, in this horn were eyes like the eyes of a man, and a mouth speaking great things.*

And Daniel 7:19–23:

> *Then I desired to know the truth about the fourth Beast, which was different from all the*

> *rest, exceedingly terrifying, with its teeth of iron and claws of bronze, and which devoured and broke in pieces and stamped what was left with its feet, and about the ten horns that were on its head, and the other horn that came up and before which three of them fell, the horn that had eyes and a mouth that spoke great things, and that seemed greater than its companions. As I looked, this horn made war with the saints and prevailed over them, until the Ancient of Days came, and judgment was given for the saints of the Most High, and the time came when the saints possessed the Kingdom. Thus he said: "As for the fourth Beast, there shall be a fourth Kingdom on Earth, which shall be different from all the Kingdoms, and it shall devour the whole Earth, and trample it down, and break it to pieces."*

Next, let's look at Daniel 8:19–27:

> *He said, "Behold, I will make known to you what shall be at the latter end of the indignation, for it refers to the appointed time of the end. As for the ram that you saw with the two horns, these are the kings of Media and Persia. And the goat is the king of Greece. And the great horn between his eyes is the first king. As for the horn that was broken, in place of which four others arose, four Kingdoms shall arise from his nation, but not with his power. And at the latter end of their Kingdom, when the transgressors*

have reached their limit, a king of bold face, one who understands riddles, shall arise. His power shall be great—but not by his own power; and he shall cause fearful destruction and shall succeed in what he does, and destroy mighty men and the people who are the saints. By his cunning he shall make deceit prosper under his hand, and in his own mind he shall become great. Without warning he shall destroy many. And he shall even rise up against the Prince of princes, and he shall be broken—but by no human hand. The vision of the evenings and the mornings that has been told is true, but seal up the vision, for it refers to many days from now." And I, Daniel, was overcome and lay sick for some days. Then I rose and went about the king's business, but I was appalled by the vision and did not understand it.

Now we can understand this last kingdom.

- There is no information concerning the Roman Empire. All the visions and dreams recorded by Daniel jump from the third empire, which is the Grecian Empire, to the fourth empire of the Antichrist at the end of the age.
- It will be strong as iron (Daniel 2:40).
- It will be partly iron and partly clay (Daniel 2:41).
- It will be a divided kingdom (Daniel 2:41).
- People will not remain united (Daniel 2:43).
- It will be different from all former beasts, and it will have ten horns representing ten nations (Daniel 7:7, 23).

- The king uprooted three of the ten horns (Daniel 7:8).
- The king crushed and devoured his victims (Daniel 7:19).
- The king waged war against the saints (Daniel 7:21).
- The vision concerned the time of the end (Daniel 8:19).
- The king's strength will not be by his own power, for the Antichrist will have been possessed by Satan, the dragon (Daniel 8:24).
- He will destroy mighty men and the holy people (Daniel 8:24).

Now, let us look at what information we can glean from the book of Revelation.

> *And another sign appeared in heaven: behold, a great red dragon, with seven heads and ten horns, and on his heads seven diadems. His tail swept down a third of the stars of heaven and cast them to the Earth. And the dragon stood before the woman who was about to give birth, so that when she bore her child he might devour it. She gave birth to a male child, one who is to rule all the nations with a rod of iron, but her child was caught up to God and to his throne, and the woman fled into the wilderness, where she has a place prepared by God, in which she is to be nourished for 1,260 days. Now war arose in heaven, Michael and his angels fighting against the dragon. And the dragon and his angels fought back, but he was defeated and*

> *there was no longer any place for them in heaven. And the great dragon was thrown down, that ancient serpent, who is called the devil and Satan, the deceiver of the whole world—he was thrown down to the Earth, and his angels were thrown down with him.*
>
> **Revelation 12:3–9**

We see an enormous red dragon, which John identifies as the devil himself cast out of heaven. Revelation 13:1–9 (KJV) gives us more information about this beast:

> *And I stood upon the sand of the sea, and saw a beast rise up out of the sea, having seven heads and ten horns, and upon his horns ten crowns, and upon his heads the name of blasphemy. And the beast which I saw was like unto a leopard, and his feet were as the feet of a bear, and his mouth as the mouth of a lion: and the dragon gave him his power, and his seat, and great authority. And I saw one of his heads as it were wounded to death; and his deadly wound was healed: and all the world wondered after the beast. And they worshipped the dragon which gave power unto the beast: and they worshipped the beast, saying, Who is like unto the beast? who is able to make war with him? And there was given unto him a mouth speaking great things and blasphemies; and power was given unto him to continue forty and two months. And he opened his mouth in blasphemy against God, to blaspheme his name, and his tabernacle,*

and them that dwell in heaven. And it was given unto him to make war with the saints, and to overcome them: and power was given him over all kindreds, and tongues, and nations. And all that dwell upon the Earth shall worship him, whose names are not written in the book of life of the Lamb slain from the foundation of the world. If any man have an ear, let him hear.

Satan gave *his power*, *his authority*, and *his throne* to the Antichrist by possessing him (remember how Jesus cast the demons out of several individuals in His earthly ministry). People who are not Christians will have a demonic spirit dwelling inside their hearts. See my book *God's Agenda: Past, Present, and Future* for more information.

We see a beast rising out of the sea, meaning the beast rises from among the masses of people inhabiting the earth. This beast has the same attributes as the first three beasts of Daniel's prophecy. The Babylonian Empire was *like a lion* (Daniel 7:4). The second beast, the Medo-Persian Empire, *was like a bear* (Daniel 7:5). The third beast, the Grecian Empire, *was like a leopard* (Daniel 7:6). The beast John saw represents the last beast, the fourth of Daniel's prophecy, which has all the characteristics of the first three combined. The next vision John has of this beast is in Revelation 17:3–18:

And he carried me away in the Spirit into a wilderness, and I saw a woman sitting on a scarlet beast that was full of blasphemous names, and it had seven heads and ten horns. The woman was arrayed in purple and scarlet, and adorned with gold and jewels and pearls, holding in her hand a golden cup full of abominations and the impurities of her sexual immorality. And on her forehead was written a name of mystery: "Babylon the great, mother of prostitutes and of Earth's abominations." And I saw the woman, drunk with the blood of the saints, the blood of the martyrs of Jesus. When I saw her, I marveled greatly. But the angel said to me, "Why do you marvel? I will tell you the mystery of the woman, and of the beast with seven heads and ten horns that carries her. The beast that you saw was, and is not, and is about to rise from the bottomless pit and go to destruction. And the dwellers on Earth whose names have not been written in the book of life from the foundation of the world will marvel to see the beast, because it was and is not and is to come. This calls for a mind with wisdom: the seven heads are seven mountains on which the woman is seated; they are also seven kings, five of whom have fallen, one is, the other has not yet come, and when he does come he must remain only a little while. As for the beast that was and is not, it is an eighth but it belongs to the seven, and it goes to destruction. And the ten horns that you saw are ten kings who have not yet received royal power, but they are to receive authority as kings for one hour, together with

The Fourth Beast Empire

the beast. These are of one mind and hand over their power and authority to the beast. They will make war on the Lamb, and the Lamb will conquer them, for he is Lord of lords and King of kings, and those with him are called and chosen and faithful." And the angel said to me, "The waters that you saw, where the prostitute is seated, are peoples and multitudes and nations and languages. And the ten horns that you saw, they and the beast will hate the prostitute. They will make her desolate and naked, and devour her flesh and burn her up with fire, for God has put it into their hearts to carry out his purpose by being of one mind and handing over their royal power to the beast, until the words of God are fulfilled. And the woman that you saw is the great city that has dominion over the kings of the Earth."

We now have all the information needed to assess what is happening during the time of this fourth beast.

Let us first look at some of these empires. Daniel revealed the identity of three of them: the Babylonian, Medo-Persian, and Grecian. John, in Revelation 17:10, describes them as "five of whom have fallen, one is, the other has not yet come." We can now understand that this "one is" refers to the Roman Empire of John's day. That places the Roman Empire as the sixth in the list of empires that arise on the earth.

Working from this information, we can determine the list as follows:

1.	The Egyptian Empire	
2.	The Assyrian Empire	
3.	The Babylonian Empire*	five fallen empires
4.	The Medo-Persian Empire*	
5.	The Grecian Empire*	
6.	The Roman Empire	one that is
7.	The Ottoman Empire	
8.	The empire of the beast, the Antichrist*	"not yet come"

*The four beasts that are referred to by the angel in Daniel 7:17.

Daniel's vision of the empires jumps from the Grecian to the "not yet come" empire, the seventh in the list, that evolves or brings forth the eighth empire of the Antichrist.

The sixth Roman Empire had its beginnings before the fall of the fifth or the Grecian Empire in 63 BCE. We know in looking at the history of the Roman Empire that the Western Roman Empire had its demise in about 476 CE. The Eastern portion of the Roman Empire had a gradual decline. The Ottoman Empire captured Constantinople in 1453 CE, bringing to an end the Eastern Roman Empire, then known as the Byzantine Empire.

Many end-time scholars and prophets of our day teach and preach a reappearance of this Roman Empire. Does it really meet the evidence as seen in the Bible?

First, let us look at the evidence of the first five empires appearing on the earth as they pertain to this study. Most scholars agree the first two empires on the list would be the Egyptian and the Assyrian empires. These empires rose extremely early in the dawn of civilization, at a time

The Fourth Beast Empire

when God was calling Abraham out of idolatry to form a people for Himself. Biblically, we understand these two empires were oppressive to God's people. They sought their destruction as a nation, but there was never any mention of them as being "beast empires."

The next three empires Daniel prophecies about are a continuation of evil empires oppressive to God's people. One would rise and fall, and another would arise and take its place. This pattern would occur all the way through the Roman Empire with no delay between the fall of one and the rise of another.

Now, are we to understand that the Roman Empire, whose fall finally occurred in 1453 CE, is the empire that is revived at the end-time, after 600+ years of nonexistence? If we study Scripture, it does not seem logical that a delay of that magnitude would occur.

Jesus tells John in Revelation 1:1–3,

> *The revelation of Jesus Christ, which God gave him to show to his servants the things that must soon take place. He made it known by sending his angel to his servant John, who bore witness to the word of God and to the testimony of Jesus Christ, even to all that he saw. Blessed is the one who reads aloud the words of this prophecy, and blessed are those who hear, and who keep what is written in it, for the time is near.*

Is it reasonable that Jesus would say it "must soon take place," if indeed it would be over 600+ years in the future

God's End-Time Puzzle

without continuity, with the "not yet come" empire having not yet taken place? I do not think so.

What happened? First, Daniel tells us that this fourth beast empire rising on the earth would be *different*. We understand this fourth beast rises out of the seventh in the list of empires we know about and that it would rise following the fall of the Roman Empire.

Was there any event following the fall of the Roman Empire that would cause us to take notice of it as being this seventh empire? The only thing we know about its rise is that it will be "different," and as John says, "he must remain for a little while." Some may say that John was referring to kings, not kingdoms, but we must understand what the angel told John in Revelation 17:9–10.

> *This calls for a mind with wisdom: the seven heads are seven mountains on which the woman is seated; they are also seven kings, five of whom have fallen, one is, the other has not yet come, and when he does come he must remain only a little while.*

The angel equates the seven hills with the seven kingdoms as being one and the same with the seven kings. The kings are the leaders of the seven kingdoms.

How did the first six empires rule? The first six kingdoms, or empires, all had a desire to rule the world. Their efforts were always by military might or by subjugating their foe with the promise of annihilation if they would not surrender to their power.

The Fourth Beast Empire

How will this seventh empire be different? This empire will appear with a different agenda: it will arise with military might, but its goal will be for you to change your allegiance from your God to its god. Its agenda is to rule the world spiritually. Convert or die. Its agenda is not to rule a nation by politics but by religion. If successful, this kingdom would have followers in every nation in the whole world—a worldwide empire.

I believe this seventh empire is Islam, an empire based on religion; Islam was the foundation of the Ottoman Empire.

- Its desire is for the whole world to worship Allah.
- Its domain is in every nation on the earth.
- Its devices are lies and deceit.
- It is militarily active through *jihad*.
- It is demonically controlled.
- It now rules nations by Sharia law.
- Islam survived the fall of the Ottoman Empire.
- National borders cannot define this empire.

This seventh "not yet come" empire was the Ottoman Empire. Out of this empire will emerge the fourth beast that will control a coalition of ten Islamic nations that will bring forth the *little horn* of Daniel's prophecy, the Antichrist, which is the eighth kingdom but the fourth beast, the last one who goes to his destruction. The Ottoman Empire ceased to be in 1923. However, the religious faction, the Islamists, have survived and are prevalent in most of the Middle East. Islam is the kingdom of the beast (Antichrist).

We notice throughout Scripture that this great red dragon with seven heads and ten horns only has seven heads; these seven heads are the seven kingdoms that arise on the earth—the seventh kingdom being the religious kingdom of Islam—all under the control of the dragon's (Satan's) demonic influence. But now we see an eighth kingdom. What can we make of this? The eighth kingdom (the fourth beast) is none other than the whole dragon (Satan), as he now indwells the Antichrist with all his power and authority. This fourth beast kingdom has also embodied all the attributes of all the beasts before it because Satan is in total control of the Antichrist. Satan's demonic princes were behind all these beast kingdoms, as we note in Daniel 10:12–13, 20–21:

> *Then he said to me, "Fear not, Daniel, for from the first day that you set your heart to understand and humbled yourself before your God, your words have been heard, and I have come because of your words. The prince of the Kingdom of Persia withstood me twenty-one days, but Michael, one of the chief princes, came to help me, for I was left there with the kings of Persia." [...] Then he said, "Do you know why I have come to you? But now I will return to fight against the prince of Persia; and when I go out, behold, the prince of Greece will come. But I will tell you what is inscribed in the book of truth: there is none who contends by my side against these except Michael, your prince."*

The Fourth Beast Empire

The Antichrist, indwelt by Satan, has now become the great red dragon with seven heads, ten horns, and seven diadems on his head. The pieces are now in place to give us a picture of this important end-time player:

The reason I reject the revived Roman Empire is that the seventh kingdom to arrive on the earth evolves to bring about the eighth empire (the fourth beast kingdom) of the Antichrist.

1. All kingdoms involved in the sequence of kingdoms up to and involving the Roman Empire have existed only to be defeated by the next empire to reign.
2. John says in Revelation 17:8 that "it was and is not," indicating that this last empire to come had already existed, "it was," and the Roman Empire, which was then in existence (the sixth in the line of empires), is not the empire that will be revived to be the kingdom of the Antichrist.
3. The eastern division of the Roman Empire existed until 1453, when it was defeated by the Ottoman Empire.
4. Now, after 600+ years without a kingdom in view, do we still expect the Roman Empire to be revived and bring forth the kingdom of the Antichrist?
5. I believe the eighth empire will arrive through the efforts of the seventh empire, which I believe is Islam: the *different* kind of empire that was founded under Islamic law. The Ottoman Empire, the political arm of Islam, was defeated in 1922; it is gone, but the Islamic religious faction lives on. I believe the Antichrist will arise out of this Islamic element.

Points to Ponder
1. Who is the fourth beast?
2. How does it come about?
3. Who is its king?

13

Investigating Current End-time Beliefs

We have looked at information relating to the end-time from the Old Testament times, before Jesus revealed to John the events leading up to the point of Jesus coming to set up His millennial kingdom. We now turn to the book of Revelation to put together the puzzle of the end-time.

How and when do these events recorded by John occur? Several questions arise regarding the various beliefs and doctrines. Many are preached as "Gospel truth," but are they?

These *assumptions* and doctrines are:

- The revived Roman Empire is the end-time empire bringing forth the eighth empire of the Antichrist, already discussed in chapter 12.
- The church is raptured at the last trumpet (the post-tribulation theory) (chapter 14).
- The tribulation is seven years (chapter 15).
- Christ's return is imminent (chapter 17).

- The seven years of tribulation are all God's wrath (chapter 20).
- John's calling to heaven is a picture of the rapture (chapter 20).
- Seals are removed to allow events to follow (chapter 21).
- The rapture is before the tribulation (chapters 28, 30).
- There are 144,000 Jews sealed to be evangelists (chapter 31).
- The trumpet and bowls are separate judgments (chapter 34).

These assumptions, when all put into one doctrine of the end-time, produce a false idea of what is really going on. These assumptions lead us to believe that we don't need to be concerned about what God is doing, as we are really going to be raptured into heaven before it all begins. One huge problem: it's wrong. According to the Scriptures, you will be here when:

- the seven-year covenant is signed;
- the new temple is built in Jerusalem;
- they start their sacrificial offerings in the temple;
- Gog invades Israel, destroying the temple and Jerusalem;
- the Antichrist is revealed, claiming that he is God;
- the false prophet shows up;
- the Israelites must flee for their lives;
- God puts forth the signs predicting the day of the Lord's wrath.

Investigating Current End-time Beliefs

Read on: you will understand that you must be ready for what's coming before Christ returns to gather His church.

14
The Last Trumpet

Behold! I tell you a mystery. We shall not all sleep, but we shall all be changed, in a moment, in the twinkling of an eye, at the last trumpet. For the trumpet will sound, and the dead will be raised imperishable, and we shall be changed.

1 Corinthians 15:51–52

Immediately after the tribulation of those days the sun will be darkened, and the moon will not give its light, and the stars will fall from heaven, and the powers of the heavens will be shaken. Then will appear in heaven the sign of the Son of Man, and then all the tribes of the Earth will mourn, and they will see the Son of Man coming on the clouds of heaven with power and great glory. And he will send out his angels with a loud trumpet call, and they will gather his elect from the four winds, from one end of heaven to the other.

Matthew 24:29–31

There has been much said about these two scriptures in defending the pre-tribulation viewpoint. The pre-tribulation movement asserts that the letter to the Corinthians refers to the last *series* of trumpets and not to the last trumpet of that series. Their viewpoint also contends that Jesus, in Matthew 24, refers not to the *rapture of the church* but to His *return to the earth* to fight the battle of Armageddon. They claim that the Matthew 24 scripture is written to the Jews and, therefore, is not pertinent to the church. On the other hand, the post-tribulation movement holds the position that Matthew 24 refers to the rapture and that the Corinthians passage refers to the last trumpet of the seven trumpet judgments of Revelation.

So, we can have directly opposite viewpoints concerning this extremely momentous event in the future history of the church. One says we do not go through the tribulation, while the other says we do.

Whose viewpoint is correct, and whose is incorrect? Scripture will tell us if we are willing to accept the evidence of its text. Let us see what the text of Scripture has to say to put this difference to rest.

Jesus shows us in verse 29 that "immediately after the tribulation of those days," the sign that Joel prophesied would occur takes place.

Jesus is referring here to the "Great Tribulation" He referred to earlier in His dialog concerning the abomination of desolation. It is only after this "Great Tribulation" that the signs will appear, as we see in Joel 2:31: "The sun shall be turned to darkness, and the moon to blood, *before the great and awesome day of the LORD comes.*"

Jesus indicates the tribulation ends with the term "after" (verse 29) but only for the elects' (believers') sake. Remember Jesus also said in Matthew 24:21–22:

> *For then there will be great tribulation, such as has not been from the beginning of the world until now, no, and never will be. And if those days had not been cut short, no human being would be saved. But for the sake of the elect those days will be cut short.*

How will "those days" be shortened? By the rapture!

What do we understand concerning the *day of the Lord*? Is it not the day that God pours out His wrath? If so, then Jesus has revealed that the tribulation and God's wrath are not one and the same. The tribulation occurs and ends for the *elects' sake before* God's wrath occurs, as stated by Joel.

The idea presented by the pre-tribulation movement that the tribulation is God's wrath is disproven by Jesus's own words. It follows that their ideas concerning the last trumpet can be discounted as just a moot point.

Now we turn attention to 1 Corinthians 15:52, "at the last trumpet." How does this fit with other scriptures?

First, in Matthew 24:31, Jesus ends his dialog concerning the end without ever mentioning God's wrath. Why? Was it that to the disciples, the gathering of the elect was the end of the matter and that, at that point, they might not be able to handle the revelation concerning God's wrath?

Second, Paul's scripture in 2 Thessalonians 1:5–10 (NIV) says,

> *All this is evidence that God's judgment is right, and as a result you will be counted worthy of the Kingdom of God, for which you are suffering. God is just: He will pay back trouble to those who trouble you and give relief to you who are troubled, and to us as well. This will happen when the Lord Jesus is revealed from heaven in blazing fire with his powerful angels. He will punish those who do not know God and do not obey the gospel of our Lord Jesus. They will be punished with everlasting destruction and shut out from the presence of the Lord [no access] and from the majesty of his power on the day he comes to be glorified in his holy people and to be marveled at among all those who have believed. This includes you, because you believed our testimony to you.*

Paul reveals here that the rapture and God's wrath occur on the very same day. This then seems to contradict his scripture about the last trumpet, as there are seven trumpet soundings that occur during God's wrath. How can we reconcile the differences? Both statements cannot be true. However, we know that Scripture cannot contradict itself. How can we then understand what these scriptures mean? The understanding of at least one of these two statements is wrong. The problem is not Scripture but how we understand it.

Jesus told us to look at Noah and Lot and their situations at the time when God poured out His wrath. On both occasions, God's protection and God's wrath occurred on the *same day*. This seems to mirror Paul's statement concerning wrath occurring on the same day the church is raptured.

Also, Revelation 14:14–20 says,

> *Then I looked, and behold, a white cloud, and seated on the cloud one like a son of man, with a golden crown on his head, and a sharp sickle in his hand. And another angel came out of the temple, calling with a loud voice to him who sat on the cloud, "Put in your sickle, and reap, for the hour to reap has come, for the harvest of the Earth is fully ripe." So he who sat on the cloud swung his sickle across the Earth, and the Earth was reaped. Then another angel came out of the temple in heaven, and he too had a sharp sickle. And another angel came out from the altar, the angel who has authority over the fire, and he called with a loud voice to the one who had the sharp sickle, "Put in your sickle and gather the clusters from the vine of the Earth, for its grapes are ripe." So the angel swung his sickle across the Earth and gathered the grape harvest of the Earth and threw it into the great winepress of the wrath of God. And the winepress was trodden outside the city,*

and blood flowed from the winepress, as high as a horse's bridle, for 1,600 stadia.

John has revealed to us the sequence of events between the rapture, which comes first, and God's wrath, which culminates in the last battle of Armageddon.

So, how does this reconcile with Paul's scripture concerning the last trumpet? It does not. So, we need to try and find out just what Paul was referring to when he made this statement about the last trumpet.

Let's look at trumpets in Scripture and see how they were used. The first mention of a trumpet is found in Exodus 19:13b: "When the trumpet sounds a long blast, they shall come up to the mountain."

Also, in Numbers 10:2–10, we read:

> *Make two silver trumpets. Of hammered work you shall make them, and you shall use them for summoning the congregation and for breaking camp. And when both are blown, all the congregation shall gather themselves to you at the entrance of the tent of meeting. But if they blow only one, then the chiefs, the heads of the tribes of Israel, shall gather themselves to you. When you blow an alarm, the camps that are on the east side shall set out. And when you blow an alarm the second time, the camps that are on the south side shall set out. An alarm is to be blown whenever they are to set out. But when the assembly is to be gathered together, you shall blow a long blast, but you shall not sound an alarm.*

And the sons of Aaron, the priests, shall blow the trumpets. The trumpets shall be to you for a perpetual statute throughout your generations. And when you go to war in your land against the adversary who oppresses you, then you shall sound an alarm with the trumpets, that you may be remembered before the Lord *your God, and you shall be saved from your enemies. On the day of your gladness also, and at your appointed feasts and at the beginnings of your months, you shall blow the trumpets over your burnt offerings and over the sacrifices of your peace offerings. They shall be a reminder of you before your God: I am the* Lord *your God.*

In Joshua 6:4–5a, we read:

Seven priests shall bear seven trumpets of rams' horns before the ark. On the seventh day you shall march around the city seven times, and the priests shall blow the trumpets. And when they make a long blast with the ram's horn, when you hear the sound of the trumpet, then all the people shall shout with a great shout, and the wall of the city will fall down flat.

These, and many other passages, make it clear that the primary purpose of trumpets was to announce what people were to do. The trumpets are blown with different types of sound and lengths of the blast. The ram's horn (the *shofar*) is also a trumpet.

There were five specifically different types of calls used by the shofar, each one used for a different purpose.

1. *Teki'ah*, a long blast (Numbers 10:3).
2. *Shevarim*, three broken blasts (Numbers 10:5).
3. *Teru'ah*, nine short blasts (Numbers 10:9).
4. *Teki'ah Gedolah*, a very long blast (Exodus 19:16, 19).
5. *Shevarim Teru'ah*, three broken blasts followed by nine short blasts.

The *teki'ah gedolah* is an extremely long blast blown for the purpose of assembling the congregation to the tent of meeting or the temple. It was also used in the announcement of the coming of the king. This is probably the blast that will be produced for the rapture of the church when Jesus comes in the clouds to meet the church in the air.

Paul evidently used the "last trumpet" wording because it would be the last time the trumpet would sound for the gathering of the church. For the church, there would be no more trumpet soundings. The soundings that would follow would be for the purpose of announcing God's wrath from which the church will be absent.

The "last trumpet" statement in 1 Corinthians 15:52 is probably referring to the Feast of Trumpets, of which the congregation would be aware. The Jewish community observes the Feast of Trumpets beginning on the first day of the seventh month and lasting for ten days. This day is also the first day of the Jewish civil, or fiscal, year.

The Last Trumpet

The feast, known as *Rosh HaShanah*, is celebrated by blowing the shofar, or ram's horn, over a hundred times throughout the duration of this feast. The last blast of the shofar, known as the *teki'ah gedolah*, which translates as the "great blowing," is an extremely long blast. It is suggested that this "great blowing" was what Paul was referring to, as it is also known as the last trumpet.

The letter to the Corinthians could have been timed to coincide with this Feast of Trumpets. Whatever his letter's timing, Paul's hearers would have understood the meaning of the "last trumpet."

Points to Ponder

1. The rapture occurs after the tribulation is shortened for the elects' (believers') sake.
2. Signs will occur before God's wrath.
3. The last trumpet is the last call for the assembling of the church in the clouds.

15

The Seven-Year Tribulation

Over the last 200 years, we have been taught, and it has been ingrained in us, that there will be a seven-year tribulation. When we desire to understand the end-time, we seem to be automatically drawn to study the books of Revelation and Daniel to find answers to what this tribulation is all about. We seem to want to limit the tribulation to this last seven-year period of the age before Christ comes to set up His kingdom. We want to take everything occurring past Revelation 4 and place it within this seven-year period. Nowhere in Scripture is there any reference to a seven-year tribulation. So, why the assumption?

The truth is the church has always been in tribulation from the beginning and will be until Christ comes back to set up His millennial reign on the earth. Just ask those around the world who are being persecuted for their faith if they are or are not in tribulation.

Daniel 9:24–27 is where they get the idea this last week of his prophecy is the seven-year tribulation. Nowhere in Scripture has it ever been expressed that this is a seven-year period of tribulation. The Bible tells us, "You will have tribulation." Jesus said in John 16:33, "I have said these things to you, that in me you may have peace. In the world *you will have tribulation*. But take heart; I have overcome the world."

Moreover, Acts 14:21–22 (NIV) says,

> *They preached the good news in that city and won a large number of disciples. Then they returned to Lystra, Iconium and Antioch, strengthening the disciples and encouraging them to remain true to the faith. "We must go through many hardships to enter the Kingdom of God," they said.*

To find answers, we must look to Daniel's prophecy concerning the seventy weeks determined upon Israel.

> *Seventy weeks are decreed about your people and your holy city, to finish the transgression, to put an end to sin, and to atone for iniquity, to bring in everlasting righteousness, to seal both vision and prophet, and to anoint a most holy place. Know therefore and understand that from the going out of the word to restore and build Jerusalem to the coming of an anointed one, a prince, there shall be seven weeks. Then for sixty-two weeks it shall be built again with squares and moat, but in a troubled time. And after the sixty-two weeks,*

The Seven-Year Tribulation

> *an anointed one shall be cut off and shall have nothing. And the people of the prince who is to come shall destroy the city and the sanctuary. Its end shall come with a flood, and to the end there shall be war. Desolations are decreed. And he shall make a strong covenant with many for one week, and for half of the week he shall put an end to sacrifice and offering. And on the wing of abominations shall come one who makes desolate, until the decreed end is poured out on the desolator.*
>
> **Daniel 9:24–27**

This scripture, by and large, is properly understood in that sixty-nine weeks have been fulfilled. The clock was stopped following the Jewish rejection of Christ as their Messiah when Jesus was crucified. God then stopped the countdown of seventy weeks, leaving one week to yet be fulfilled. God then turned to the Gentiles to establish His church. So, we are now in a time we call the church age. God will, one day, restart the clock for the seventieth week of Daniel's prophecy with an event called a *covenant*. This covenant will be a seven-year covenant between the Antichrist, his beast empire, and Israel. (We studied this beast empire in chapters 11 and 12.) It is a time when God again turns His attention toward Israel. This last seven-year period is misunderstood as the tribulation. Nowhere in Scripture does it say so. Isaiah 28:15–18 tells us:

> *Because you have said, "We have made a covenant with death, and with Sheol we have an agreement, when the overwhelming whip*

> *passes through it will not come to us, for we have made lies our refuge, and in falsehood we have taken shelter"; therefore thus says the Lord* GOD, *"Behold, I am the one who has laid as a foundation in Zion, a stone, a tested stone, a precious cornerstone, of a sure foundation: 'Whoever believes will not be in haste.' And I will make justice the line, and righteousness the plumb line; and hail will sweep away the refuge of lies, and waters will overwhelm the shelter." Then your covenant with death will be annulled, and your agreement with Sheol will not stand; when the overwhelming scourge passes through, you will be beaten down by it.*

The covenant referred to in Daniel 9:27 prophecy is the same as Isaiah's prophecy of 28:15–18.

The Antichrist will not be recognized as such when Israel makes a covenant with him and his beast empire. *They will believe this covenant to be a seven-year covenant of peace when, in reality, it will be a covenant with death.* It is my understanding there will be a time of relative peace with Israel for the first three and a half years.

Daniel 9:27 (NIV) reveals to us information concerning the "abomination that causes desolation." This event is also recorded in Matthew 24:15 and is understood to be a time of the Great Tribulation beginning at the midpoint of this last week of Daniel's prophecy: "So when you see *the abomination of desolation* spoken of by the prophet Daniel, standing in the holy place (let the reader understand)."

The Seven-Year Tribulation

Matthew 24:22 also says, "And if those days had not been cut short, no human being would be saved. *But for the sake of the elect those days will be cut short.*"

Who are these "elect" Jesus refers to? Are they Christians or Jews? What does the word "elect" mean? Throughout the New Testament, whenever the word "elect" was used, it was *always* referring to believers. If we look at these end-time events, who was Jesus referring to when He used the word "elect"? Was it for the Christians or for the Jews? We must remember the Jews were not yet believers. They were, and are, still looking for their Messiah. Those days Christ said would be shortened for the sake of the elect (believers).

Jesus also said in Matthew 24:21, "For then there will be great tribulation, such as has not been from the beginning of the world until now, no, and never will be."

This verse plainly tells us that the shortened days were in a time of the Great Tribulation, which places the Christians within the time of Satan's wrath, a day that would be shortened for the elects' (believers') sake. What explanation could there be other than that Jesus was referring to the rapture? Remember: the Jews were not Christians at this point and, therefore, could not be called the "elect." Satan's time was not shortened; his allotted time would still be allowed.

These last seven years will begin with deception, a covenant of peace, in reality, a *covenant with death*.

Because you have said, "We have made a covenant with death, and with Sheol we have an agreement, when the overwhelming whip passes through it will not come to us, for we have made lies our refuge, and in falsehood we have taken shelter." [...] Then your covenant with death will be annulled, and your agreement with Sheol will not stand; when the overwhelming scourge passes through, you will be beaten down by it.

Isaiah 28:15, 18

There will be a semblance of peace for the Jews for the first three and a half years, as this covenant with death seems to indicate. Jesus declares in Matthew 24:15 that an *abomination of desolation* will take place, just as Daniel prophesied that it will occur in the *middle of the week*.

Understanding that this occurs in the middle of the week would lead us to conclude that His comment in Matthew 24:21 concerning the Great Tribulation means it would occur in the last three and a half years. Later we will find that the Antichrist is given 1,260 days (three and one-half years) once he marches into Jerusalem.

Points to Ponder

1. What is the tribulation?
2. How long is the tribulation?
3. Why are there differing views about the tribulation?
4. Why is there a Great Tribulation?
5. Why is the Great Tribulation cut short?

The Seven-Year Tribulation

DANIELS 70 WEEK PROPHECY

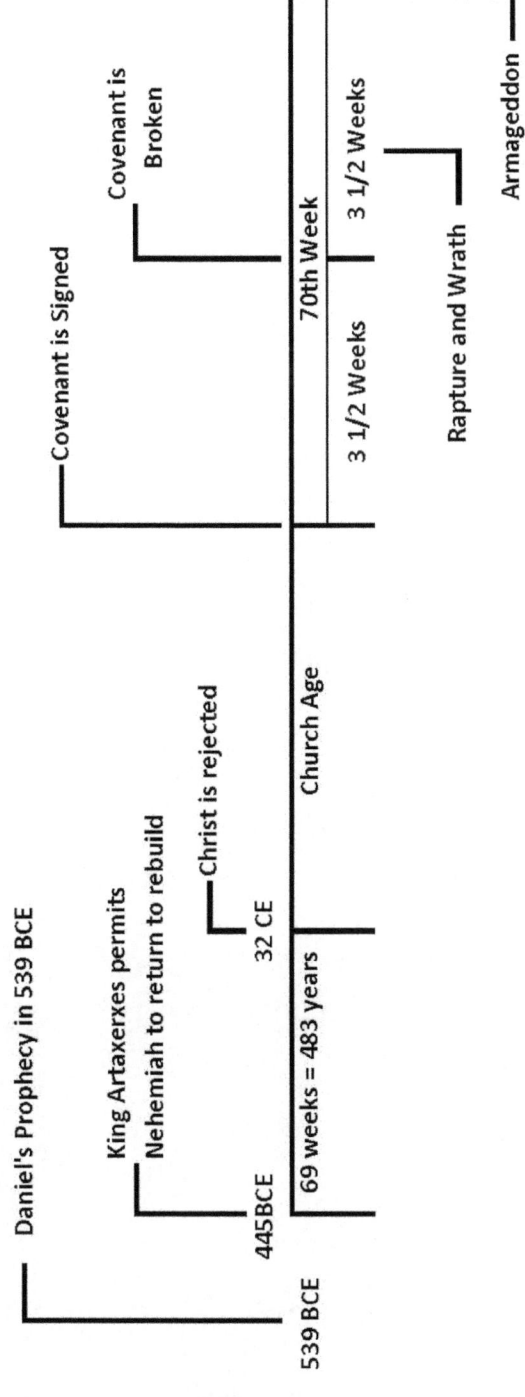

- Daniel's Prophecy in 539 BCE
- King Artaxerxes permits Nehemiah to return to rebuild
- 445 BCE
- 69 weeks = 483 years
- 32 CE
- Christ is rejected
- Church Age
- Covenant is Signed
- Covenant is Broken
- 70th Week
- 3 1/2 Weeks
- 3 1/2 Weeks
- Rapture and Wrath
- Armageddon
- 539 BCE

16

The 2,300 Evenings and Mornings

The 2,300-evenings-and-mornings vision Daniel received from the angel was not understood by him or the multitude of peoples down through the ages, the reason being that the vision was not to be understood until the time of the end.

> *It became great, even as great as the Prince of the host. And the regular burnt offering was taken away from him, and the place of his sanctuary was overthrown. And a host will be given over to it together with the regular burnt offering because of transgression, and it will throw truth to the ground, and it will act and prosper. Then I heard a holy one speaking, and another holy one said to the one who spoke, "For how long is the vision concerning the regular burnt offering, the transgression that makes desolate, and the giving over of the sanctuary and host to be*

> *trampled underfoot?" And he said to me, "For 2,300 evenings and mornings. Then the sanctuary shall be restored to its rightful state."*
>
> **Daniel 8:11–14**

Later in the same chapter, Daniel is told by the angel: "The vision of *the evenings and the mornings* that has been told is true, but *seal up the vision*, for it refers to many days from now" (verse 26).

Many believe this scripture refers to the time Antiochus Epiphanes desecrated the temple on December 25, 167 BCE. However, it appears that all these visions given to Daniel concerning the *evening and morning* sacrifices occur in the last days, and the Antiochus Epiphanes event should, therefore, only be looked at as a *shadow of the end-time*. This prophecy should then be understood as an end-time prophecy.

To understand this prophecy, we must consider everything we know about the end-time.

- We know and understand that there is a seven-year period commonly understood as the tribulation. It is divided into two sections of 1,260 days each, the latter known as the Great Tribulation.
- We know, according to what Daniel tells us, that "in the midst" of the week, the Antichrist shall cause the sacrifice and oblation to cease (Daniel 9:27).
- Daniel receives a 2,300-day prophecy that will occur during this last week. It reveals that a

sanctuary must be in existence during this period.

- Daniel 8:13 reveals a holy one asking how long it will take to fulfill the vision of what happens during this 2,300-day period concerning:
    1. "the regular burnt offering,"
    2. "the transgression that makes desolate,"
    3. and "the giving over of the sanctuary and host to be trampled underfoot."
- The answer was, "For 2,300 evenings and mornings. *Then the sanctuary shall be restored to its rightful state*" (Daniel 8:14).

Daniel 12:9–13 gives us more information:

> *He said, "Go your way, Daniel, for the words are shut up and sealed until the time of the end. Many shall purify themselves and make themselves white and be refined, but the wicked shall act wickedly. And none of the wicked shall understand, but those who are wise shall understand. And from the time that the regular burnt offering is taken away and the abomination that makes desolate is set up, there shall be 1,290 days. Blessed is he who waits and arrives at the 1,335 days. But go your way till the end. And you shall rest and shall stand in your allotted place at the end of the days."*

In these *last days*, a revelation seems to have been opened to us. Let us see if we can make sense of the few scriptures pertaining to this subject.

First, let us look at what is revealed in Daniel 8:9. It says, "Out of one of them came a little horn." Daniel was telling us the little horn (Antichrist) would come out of a division of the Grecian Empire. This Grecian Empire ceased to exist in 63 BCE. It will be the Seleucid division that produces the Antichrist. I believe this because the balance of that scripture deals with events of the Seleucid division leading up to the end.

He (Antichrist) is the one who sets all these things in motion when he approves the "covenant with death" signed by his beast kingdom and Israel (see Isaiah 28:18). It is during this covenant that all these evening and morning events take place. So, it is limited to the last week of Daniel's prophecy of 2,520 days.

We know that the Antichrist will be defeated at the end of his 1,260 allotted days from the middle of the last week.

Daniel gives us information in 12:11 that there are 1,290 days from the time the burnt offering is taken away and the abomination has been set up to the end of Satan's allotted time (the end of the week). Verse 12, which says, "Blessed is he who waits and arrives at the 1,335 days," seems to indicate that there is a forty-five-day restoration period following the end of the week.

This reveals a temple must be in existence during this last week and begins its evening and morning burnt offerings 2,300 days before the temple is restored at the end of a forty-five-day restoration period following the end of the last week of Daniel's prophecy.

The 2,300 Evenings and Mornings

It also allows us to see the temple sacrifice its offerings for 965 days before the temple is destroyed, 1,290 days before the end of the week (thirty days before the middle of the week). This also allows us to see that the temple begins its sacrifices 265 days following the signing of the covenant.

We also know that there is no temple residing in Israel at the time of this writing. It is possible that when a covenant is signed with the beast and his empire, it will permit the building of the temple. So, these are the facts we need to know and understand:

1. It is known by most scholars that there will be a temple in operation at some point during the last week of Daniel's prophecy.

2. When does the temple start its sacrificial offerings? We know from Daniel 8:14 that from the end of the restoration period after the tribulation back to the beginning of the temple sacrifices, there will be 2,300 days (265 days from the beginning of the seven-year covenant).

3. When do the sacrificial offerings cease? Again, working from the end of the restoration period and using evidence presented by the angel in Daniel 12:11–12, we find there will be 1,335 days back to when the sacrifices are abolished. Also, it seems to be that it will be 1,290 days from the end of the seven-year covenant, leaving forty-five days for the restoration.

4. When does the abomination of desolation occur? Daniel 9:27 (KJV) says,

> *And he shall confirm the covenant with many for one week: and in the midst of the week he shall cause the sacrifice and the oblation to cease, and for the overspreading of abominations he shall make it desolate, even until the consummation, and that determined shall be poured upon the desolate.*

> *The angel is telling us that some point "in the midst of the week" (i.e., not necessarily the exact midpoint) will be when the abomination of desolation occurs.*

5. What causes the sacrificial offerings to cease? Daniel 9:26 (KJV) states,

> *And after threescore and two weeks shall Messiah be cut off, but not for himself: and the people of the prince that shall come shall destroy the city and the sanctuary; and the end thereof shall be with a flood, and unto the end of the war desolations are determined.*

"The people of the prince" (i.e., not the Antichrist but his followers) will go in and destroy the city and sanctuary. I believe it is Gog who does the dirty work of the Antichrist. The Antichrist will march in later to set up the abomination of desolation spoken of by Daniel 9:27. This will probably happen when God says enough is enough and limits the Antichrist and his kingdom to only 1,260 days until his end.

I believe God has now revealed this end-time prophecy. I believe it proves we are now in the time we should be

The 2,300 Evenings and Mornings

preparing ourselves for the upcoming events of the end-time when Jesus returns to gather His elect and to pour out His wrath, defeating Satan and setting up His millennial reign.

God's End-Time Puzzle

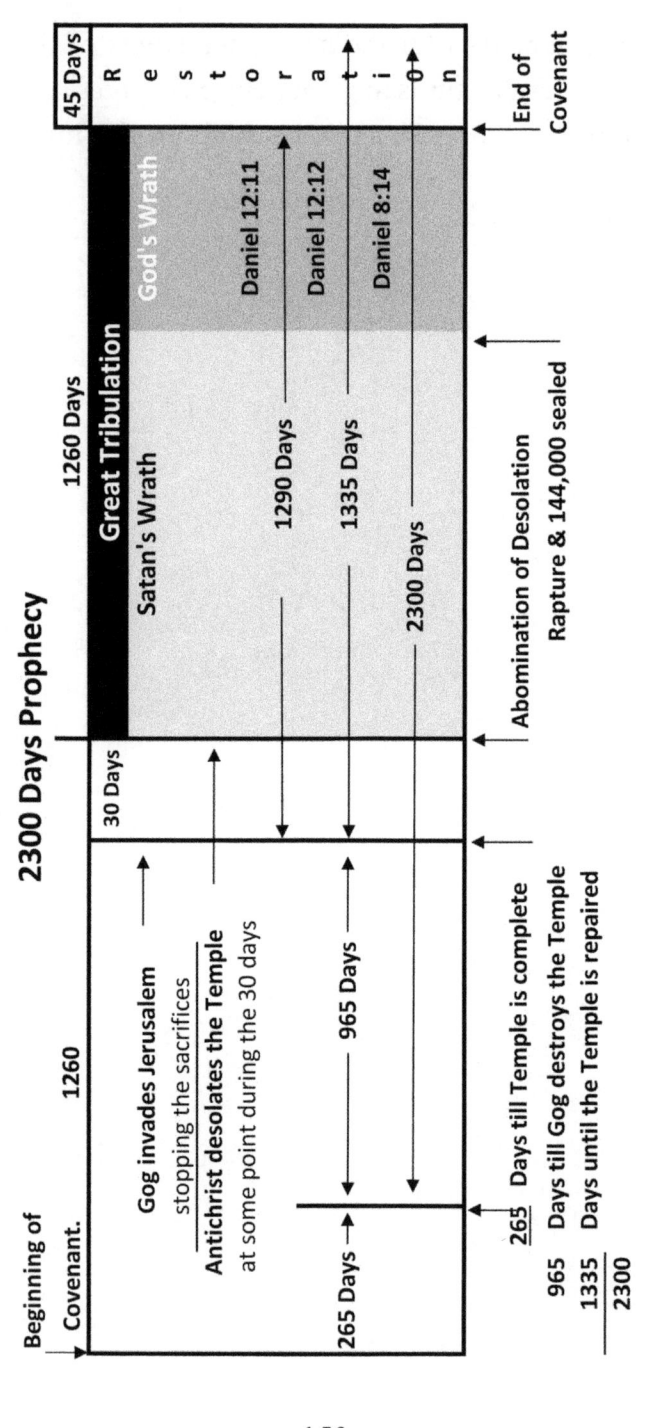

2300 Days Prophecy

Beginning of Covenant.	1260

Gog invades Jerusalem stopping the sacrifices

Antichrist desolates the Temple at some point during the 30 days

30 Days

Great Tribulation — 1260 Days

Satan's Wrath

God's Wrath

45 Days — Restoration

265 Days
965 Days
1290 Days — Daniel 12:11
1335 Days — Daniel 12:12
2300 Days — Daniel 8:14

Abomination of Desolation
Rapture & 144,000 sealed

End of Covenant

<u>265</u> Days till Temple is complete
965 Days till Gog destroys the Temple
<u>1335</u> Days until the Temple is repaired
2300

17

The Imminence of Christ's Return

Ever since the rapture-before-the-tribulation has been preached, they have been stating the rapture of the church could happen at any moment, as Christ will return as a thief in the night. They have been preaching there is nothing that needs to happen before His coming to take His bride away. "A secret calling away," they say. But is it? Does the Bible tell us of anything occurring before He comes for the church?

Joel 2:30–31 tells us,

> *And I will show wonders in the heavens and on the Earth, blood and fire and columns of smoke. The sun shall be turned to darkness, and the moon to blood, before the great and awesome day of the LORD comes.*

This scripture reveals to us that "before the great and awesome day of the Lord comes" (God's wrath), there will be a sign that all mankind will see.

God's End-Time Puzzle

Immediately after the tribulation of those days the sun will be darkened, and the moon will not give its light, and the stars will fall from heaven, and the powers of the heavens will be shaken. Then will appear in heaven the sign of the Son of Man, and then all the tribes of the Earth will mourn, and they will see the Son of Man coming on the clouds of heaven with power and great glory. And he will send out his angels with a loud trumpet call, and they will gather his elect from the four winds, from one end of heaven to the other.

Matthew 24:29–31

But in those days, after that tribulation, the sun will be darkened, and the moon will not give its light, and the stars will be falling from heaven, and the powers in the heavens will be shaken. And then they will see the Son of Man coming in clouds with great power and glory. And then he will send out the angels and gather his elect from the four winds, from the ends of the Earth to the ends of heaven.

Mark 13:24–27

And there will be signs in sun and moon and stars, and on the Earth distress of nations in perplexity because of the roaring of the sea and the waves, people fainting with fear and with foreboding of what is coming on the world. For the powers of the heavens will be shaken. And then they will see the Son of

The Imminence of Christ's Return

Man coming in a cloud with power and great glory. Now when these things begin to take place, straighten up and raise your heads, because your redemption is drawing near.

Luke 21:25–28

This event, as recorded in Matthew, Mark, and Luke, *must occur before* Christ gathers His elect (the church). Luke states, "Now when these things begin to take place, straighten up and raise your heads, because your redemption is drawing near." He is declaring to you that the rapture is now imminent. So, when does this event take place?

When he opened the sixth seal, I looked, and behold, there was a great Earthquake, and the sun became black as sackcloth, the full moon became like blood, and the stars of the sky fell to the Earth as the fig tree sheds its winter fruit when shaken by a gale. The sky vanished like a scroll that is being rolled up, and every mountain and island was removed from its place. Then the kings of the Earth and the great ones and the generals and the rich and the powerful, and everyone, slave and free, hid themselves in the caves and among the rocks of the mountains, calling to the mountains and rocks, "Fall on us and hide us from the face of him who is seated on the throne, and from the wrath of the Lamb, for the great day of their wrath has come, and who can stand?"

Revelation 6:12–17

It is apparent that when this event takes place, it gets into the minds of everybody on the earth that God's wrath is about to be poured out. This is the event Joel 2:31 says that will occur *before* the day of the Lord takes place.

Are there any other things that must take place before God's wrath is poured out?

It is evident in reading the Olivet discourse as recorded in Matthew 24 and Mark 13 that the abomination of desolation spoken of by Daniel the prophet takes place *before* God's wrath is poured out. It requires that the temple in Jerusalem must be built and in operation before Christ's return. This event occurs in the middle of the last week of Daniel's prophecy.

> *After the sixty-two "sevens," the Anointed One will be put to death and will have nothing. The people of the ruler who will come will destroy the city and the sanctuary. The end will come like a flood: War will continue until the end, and desolations have been decreed. He will confirm a covenant with many for one "seven." In the middle of the "seven" he will put an end to sacrifice and offering. And at the temple he will set up an abomination that causes desolation, until the end that is decreed is poured out on him.*
> **Daniel 9:26–27 (NIV)**

Daniel tells us that the abomination of desolation takes place "in the middle of the 'seven'" (week).

Paul tells us in 2 Thessalonians 2:1–5 (NIV),

The Imminence of Christ's Return

Concerning the coming of our Lord Jesus Christ and our being gathered to him, we ask you, brothers and sisters, not to become easily unsettled or alarmed by the teaching allegedly from us—whether by a prophecy or by word of mouth or by letter—asserting that the day of the Lord has already come. Don't let anyone deceive you in any way, for that day will not come until the rebellion occurs and the man of lawlessness is revealed, the man doomed to destruction. He will oppose and will exalt himself over everything that is called God or is worshiped, so that he sets himself up in God's temple, proclaiming himself to be God. Don't you remember that when I was with you I used to tell you these things?

God is just: He will pay back trouble to those who trouble you and give relief to you who are troubled, and to us as well. This will happen when the Lord Jesus is revealed from heaven in blazing fire with his powerful angels. He will punish those who do not know God and do not obey the gospel of our Lord Jesus. They will be punished with everlasting destruction and shut out from the presence of the Lord and from the glory of his might on the day he comes to be glorified in his holy people and to be marveled at among all those who have believed. This includes you, because you believed our testimony to you.

2 Thessalonians 1:6–10 (NIV)

God's End-Time Puzzle

Paul has shown to us that the Antichrist will be revealed *before the Lord's day* (wrath) and that the rapture will occur on the *same day* God begins to pour out His wrath.

This information, all from the Bible, reveals to us that the rapture of the church *cannot and will not happen* until after the events occurring in the middle of this last week.

The rapture is not imminent until these events begin to take place, as Luke 21:25–28 declares:

- Signs will appear before the great and awesome day of the Lord comes (Joel 2:30–31, Revelation 6:12–14).
- An abomination of desolation will occur in the middle of the last week (Daniel 9:27, Matthew 24:15).
- Then Jesus calls what follows the abomination of desolation, the Great Tribulation (Matthew 24:21).
- Then Jesus says He will cut short the Great Tribulation for the believers' sake. "And if those days had not been cut short, no human being would be saved. But for the sake of the elect those days will be cut short" (Matthew 24:22).
- Then, Jesus says, signs will appear immediately after the tribulation of those days (Matthew 24:29).
- Then the sign of the Son of Man coming on the clouds will appear (Matthew 24:30).
- Then He will send out His angels with a trumpet call to gather His elect (Matthew 24:31).
- That day will not come until "the man of lawlessness [Antichrist] is revealed" (2 Thessalonians 2:3, NIV).

The Imminence of Christ's Return

- Wrath will occur on the same day as the rapture (2 Thessalonians 2:10).

Points to Ponder

1. What did Jesus say will happen before He comes?
2. Has it happened yet?

18
The Book of Revelation

Many believe the *book of Revelation* is a divided book: the first three chapters are for the church, while chapters 4–21 are for the Jews. This, however, is an erroneous view. It is true the first three chapters are letters to the seven churches, *all Gentile in origin.* But to say Revelation after chapter three is all for the Jews is deceptive, leading the rest of us to believe it is not for us. The rest of the book of Revelation is vital for our understanding of what will happen.

> *I was in the Spirit on the Lord's Day, and I heard behind me a loud voice like a trumpet saying, "Write what you see in a book and send it to the seven churches, to Ephesus and to Smyrna and to Pergamum and to Thyatira and to Sardis and to Philadelphia and to Laodicea."*
>
> **Revelation 1:10–11**

John is instructed to write *what he sees*: he is not released from his vision until all the vision of Revelation is revealed. *Therefore, the vision is for the churches.*

The idea that means the church must have been raptured (*an assumption*) during this period because the word "church" is not included in chapters 4–21 is simply not true. The letters sent to the seven churches were sent to seven separate congregations of Christians. During the vision of Revelation 4 through 21, "churches" are not mentioned because they are not referred to as congregations of Christians but as "saints," which are individual Christians and could come from all seven congregations, not just one congregation, or from Christians the world over. The word "saints" in the New Testament always refers to individual Christians. In the book of Revelation, beyond chapter 3, we find the word "saints." "Saints" (plural) are mentioned eleven times, being individual believers, members of God's church.

Also, in Revelation 22:16, we find these words: "I, Jesus, have sent my angel to testify to you about these things for the churches. I am the root and the descendant of David, the bright morning star."

Also, in Revelation 1:19, we read: "Write therefore the things that you have seen, those that are and those that are to take place after this."

Here again, the entire testimony given to John, from beginning to the end of the entire book of Revelation, was intended for the seven churches, not part for the Jews and part for the church. If Revelation were for the Jews, it would seem the instruction to John would have been to send it to both Jewish and Gentile congregations.

The Book of Revelation

Finally, the instruction to John was to write "the things that you have seen, those that are and those that are to take place after this." The letters written to the seven churches were not only what he saw but also what Jesus told him (i.e., what he heard) to write as dictation from the Lord. What John saw was the vision before and after what he was told to write by dictation to the seven churches. Chapter 4 begins as a continuation of John's vision in the spirit and was to be included in the letters John was to write to the seven churches.

Points to Ponder
1. What does the book of Revelation reveal?
2. Who was it written to?
3. Why was it written?

19

The Seven Churches

> *The revelation of Jesus Christ, which God gave him to show to his servants the things that must soon take place. He made it known by sending his angel to his servant John, who bore witness to the word of God and to the testimony of Jesus Christ, even to all that he saw. Blessed is the one who reads aloud the words of this prophecy, and blessed are those who hear, and who keep what is written in it, for the time is near.*
>
> **Revelation 1:1–3**

We must understand that this revelation came from Jesus Christ Himself and was given to John, who, in turn, wrote down and testified to everything he saw as being revealed from God. He then makes a statement concerning what he heard and what he saw (see verse 3). This statement tells us a lot about the book of Revelation. It is a book that should be read, and the words—kept. It tells us the book was to be understood and comprehended.

It was not to be understood as some symbolic writing as to future events, although there are some symbols that are to be understood as symbols only and not as some symbolic event that cannot be understood with absolute certainty. The prophecy was to be understood, whenever possible, as "literal" events that happen exactly as John saw and wrote about them.

The "Revelation of Jesus Christ," which starts out this book, means precisely what it says. Revelation or "Revealed" is a book intended to reveal to us the unfolding of events during the end of the age, plain and simple; this book is to be understood, not by just a few but by all. See Revelation 1:3 above.

> *John to the seven churches that are in Asia: Grace to you and peace from him who is and who was and who is to come, and from the seven spirits who are before his throne, and from Jesus Christ the faithful witness, the firstborn of the dead, and the ruler of kings on Earth. To him who loves us and has freed us from our sins by his blood.*
>
> **Revelation 1:4–5**

John was in the spirit when he began to hear Jesus talking and declaring to him.

> *I was in the Spirit on the Lord's Day, and I heard behind me a loud voice like a trumpet saying, "Write what you see in a book and send it to the seven churches, to Ephesus and to Smyrna and to Pergamum and to Thyatira*

The Seven Churches

and to Sardis and to Philadelphia and to Laodicea."

Revelation 1:10–11

After this declaration to John by Jesus, he saw a vision that included seven golden lampstands and seven stars. Jesus then made known to John what these symbols were or are. The seven golden lampstands are the seven churches to which John was instructed to write. The seven stars were revealed to be the seven angels of the seven churches. We understand this to mean the ministers of the seven churches.

> *"Write therefore the things that you have seen, those that are and those that are to take place after this" (Revelation 1:19).*

Also, in Revelation 22:16, Jesus declares, "I, Jesus, have sent my angel to testify to you about these things for the churches. I am the root and the descendant of David, the bright morning star."

Notice: this *testimony* was "for the churches." There is only one meaning: it is that every word of the book of Revelation was meant "for the churches" (congregations of individual Christians).

The letters Jesus instructed John to write to the seven churches were pertinent to all churches of all ages. All the conditions represented by these individual churches are pertinent to the entire spectrum of church history down through the ages.

Jesus has told us everything we need to know concerning these seven churches.

Read Revelation, chapters 2 and 3.

Most of what Jesus had to say about these seven churches was about what their spiritual condition was at that time. He warned some about what could or would happen to them in the future.

Jesus reveals to all that:
- He knows their works and what is going on.
- He knows their successes and failures.
- He knows Satan is also working in their midst.
- He admonishes them to repent.
- He says there are consequences if they do not repent.
- He says that if they overcome, they will have a reward.

These words of Jesus tell us all we need to know. Nothing could be hidden from Christ knowing what was going on in the churches, their good works, their bad works, their failures, and their successes—everything.

He knows who we are, what we are, and why we do the things we do, whether for God or ourselves.

These letters were intended for circulation to each and every church mentioned, possibly to all churches everywhere.

We must be faithful in all situations; this admonition should be a warning to all of us that we must "overcome"

The Seven Churches

to enjoy eternal life. We must be victorious in our walk with Christ.

The seven churches represent the attitudes, aspirations, failures, desires, tribulations, successes, and willingness of all the churches in every city, town, and village of every nation, language, and culture. He knows our heart and dedication and whether we are hot or cold in our love and service to Him.

Some have preached and taught these seven churches represent seven church ages. We, as people, have a habit of reading into Scripture something that is just not there to facilitate our assumptions of what "should be," not just "what is." Let us take the Scripture at face value and not what we think it is trying to say.

Jesus told John to write to the seven churches "what is, what was and what will be." This information about the seven churches was the "what is." Let's leave it at that. It is what it is…in every age!

Points to Ponder

1. What does God's message to the seven churches reveal?
2. Is the message God wants to be known for the Jews only or for all?
3. What is He really trying to tell us?
4. Are we to understand what is written?

20
John Is Called into Heaven

The idea that Revelation 4:1 is a snapshot of the rapture has many problems.

> *After this I looked, and behold, a door standing open in heaven! And the first voice, which I had heard speaking to me like a trumpet, said, "Come up here, and I will show you what must take place after this." At once I was in the Spirit, and behold, a throne stood in heaven, with one seated on the throne.*
>
> **Revelation 4:1–2**

Some believe that this scripture is a picture of the rapture. I see no real evidence anywhere in this scripture that would lead me to that conclusion. Remember the golden rule of Scripture, "if the plain sense makes sense, it's the right sense." The common sense of this scripture should tell us that John was called into heaven for the purpose of showing John "what must take place after this" (in the future), plain and simple.

So, what did John see when he was caught up into heaven, directly into God's throne room? He saw what the throne room looked like with the elders and living creatures (beasts) worshipping God. He then sees in chapter 5 what, I believe, was the reason he was brought into heaven. It was to reveal to him the events that would happen *in the future*, from the opening of seal one until Christ would be crowned King of kings and Lord of lords, and Satan cast into the lake of fire forever and ever.

The key to understanding the book of Revelation is having the right understanding of this event (John being called into heaven).

If you look at this event as a picture of the rapture, then...

- You conclude that the seal removals are entirely after the rapture of the church.
- It shuts the door on the significance of the rest of the book of Revelation following this event. It is not for the church; it's for Israel.
- It forces all events of Revelation as coming after the rapture.
- It minimizes the importance of events from the time of John until after the rapture.
- The rapture images beyond chapter 4 occur after God's wrath has started and, therefore, must all be a part of the tribulation.

Claiming that John represents the raptured church shuts the door to a proper understanding of the book of Revelation. It places the timing of everything John saw in his vision as occurring after the rapture. Therefore, the seals are all opened after the rapture, so they must be God's wrath and the start of the seven-year tribulation. They say it is Satan who rides the white horse of seal one and that he comes as a deceiver. That goes against what the Scriptures are telling us. They then say the church is not mentioned after chapter 3, so they are not present during the events John saw after he was taken into heaven. They are not mentioned because the reference is not to congregations of people (churches) but to individual people (saints).

We dealt extensively with the seven-year tribulation in chapter 15. Realizing that we, as Christians and Jews, have always been in tribulation, we must only consider the Great Tribulation as three and one-half years.

> *So when you see the abomination of desolation spoken of by the prophet Daniel, standing in the holy place (let the reader understand), then let those who are in Judea flee to the mountains. Let the one who is on the housetop not go down to take what is in his house, and let the one who is in the field not turn back to take his cloak. And alas for women who are pregnant and for those who are nursing infants in those days! Pray that your flight may not be in winter or on a Sabbath. For then there will be great tribulation, such as has not been from the beginning of the world until now, no, and never will be.*
>
> **Matthew 24:15–21**

Jesus, in His discourse, has revealed many things leading up to this "abomination of desolation" that would place the opening of these seals as starting before this Great Tribulation (see Matthew 24:1–14). Daniel reveals to us just when this *abomination of desolation* occurs.

> *And he shall make a strong covenant with many for one week, and for half of the week [three and one-half years] he shall put an end to sacrifice and offering. And on the wing of abominations shall come one who makes desolate, until the decreed end is poured out on the desolator.*
>
> **Daniel 9:27**

Jesus tells us, "When you see the *abomination of desolation* […] standing in the holy place (let the reader understand), […] then there will be *great tribulation*."

> *Now concerning the coming of our Lord Jesus Christ and our being gathered together to him, we ask you, brothers, not to be quickly shaken in mind or alarmed, either by a spirit or a spoken word, or a letter seeming to be from us, to the effect that the day of the Lord has come. Let no one deceive you in any way. For that day will not come, unless the rebellion comes first, and the man of lawlessness is revealed, the son of destruction, who opposes and exalts himself against every so-called god or object of worship, so that he takes his seat in the temple of God, proclaiming himself to be God. Do you not remember that when*

John Is Called into Heaven

I was still with you I told you these things? And you know what is restraining him now so that he may be revealed in his time. For the mystery of lawlessness is already at work. Only he who now restrains it will do so until he is out of the way. And then the lawless one will be revealed, whom the Lord Jesus will kill with the breath of his mouth and bring to nothing by the appearance of his coming. The coming of the lawless one is by the activity of Satan with all power and false signs and wonders.

2 Thessalonians 2:1–9

Paul says that the day of the Lord (God's wrath) will not come "unless the rebellion comes first, and the man of lawlessness is revealed, the son of destruction." The day "the man of lawlessness is revealed" is the day the Antichrist marches into Jerusalem and declares himself to be God. The *abomination of desolation* occurs in the middle of the week. It is the day that starts the Great Tribulation, the last three and one-half years before Christ sets up His kingdom. The day of the Lord (God's wrath) will come at some point *after* this Great Tribulation starts.

Paul also reveals to us that the rapture will occur on the same day God's wrath begins.

Since indeed God considers it just to repay with affliction those who afflict you, and to grant relief to you who are afflicted as well as to us, when the Lord Jesus is revealed from heaven with his mighty angels in flaming fire,

> *inflicting vengeance on those who do not know God and on those who do not obey the gospel of our Lord Jesus. They will suffer the punishment of eternal destruction, away from the presence of the Lord and from the glory of his might, when he comes on that day to be glorified in his saints, and to be marveled at among all who have believed, because our testimony to you was believed.*
>
> **2 Thessalonians 1:6–10**

Jesus also revealed to us in Matthew 24:37–39 and in Luke 17:27 that the rapture would occur on the same day God's wrath would be poured out. He told us, "For as were the days of Noah, so will be the coming of the Son of Man." Noah entered the ark on the same day God began to pour out His wrath (see Genesis 7:13–16). Luke also included Lot's departure from Sodom on the same day that God's wrath was poured out (Luke 17:29). These were points of reference Jesus told us to look at.

Points to Ponder

1. Why was John called into heaven?
2. Was John a picture of the rapture?
3. What did he see?

21

The Scroll

Understanding the End-Time

The scroll reveals a sequential order of events that must take place for Christ to reacquire His rightful ownership of planet Earth. It is the "road map" to the millennial reign of Christ.

> *Then I saw in the right hand of him who was seated on the throne a scroll written within and on the back, sealed with seven seals. And I saw a mighty angel proclaiming with a loud voice, "Who is worthy to open the scroll and break its seals?" And no one in heaven or on Earth or under the Earth was able to open the scroll or to look into it, and I began to weep loudly because no one was found worthy to open the scroll or to look into it. And one of the elders said to me, "Weep no more; behold, the Lion of the tribe of Judah, the Root of David, has conquered, so that he can open the scroll and its seven seals."*
>
> **Revelation 5:1–5**

This scripture reveals very important elements in understanding the events of the end-time. They are sequential and lead up to Christ defeating evil and gaining His rightful position as King of kings and Lord of lords.

We see, in verse one, God sitting on His throne, a scroll in His hand with writing on both sides. A mighty angel is looking for someone to open the scroll but finds none. Already several questions arise concerning this scroll. What is the origin of this scroll? Who wrote it and why? What are its contents? What happened that caused the necessity for its opening? And many more questions?

Before we attempt to answer these questions, we need to look at the usage of a sealed scroll in the ancient world. Scrolls had many uses, such as sacred texts of the Bible, official documents of business and national importance. Scrolls were also used for last wills and testaments. Some scrolls did not need to be sealed as they were used daily, such as biblical scrolls. Some scrolls were *sealed* and protected from viewing until something happened, causing the removal of the seal so the scroll could be opened and read.

The scroll in Revelation 5 was of this type. It was sealed with *seven seals*. A seal's removal could only occur because an event or condition caused its removal. It was not to be removed in order to allow something to happen. First the event, then the seal's removal.

In the case of a last will and testament that was sealed, it would require the death of the testator before the seal's removal. Another condition could have been that all

The Scroll

living relatives of the testator be present before the seal's removal. Other conditions may be present for any number of reasons. The fact is, conditions must be met before the seal's removal.

We see God holding the scroll and the angel looking for someone who has the right to open the seals. *A condition written on the outside of the scroll must have occurred, causing the angel to look for someone who had the right to remove the first seal.* Jesus, recognized as "the Lion of the tribe of Judah," was found to have the right and authority to remove the seals from the scroll. We will learn as we complete the study that Jesus had the right to administer the wrath events recorded on the inside of the scroll. The events causing the removal of the seals are not God's wrath. They are most likely events brought on by Satan and his minions in order to rule the world and be worshiped as God.

The idea presented by some that the removal of a seal allows an event to occur is just not true. The seals are placed on a scroll for a reason. That reason must be satisfied before its removal, first the reason, then the removal of the seal. Seven seals on the scroll seem to indicate seven events need to take place for their removal.

First, verse 1 refers to a scroll sealed with seven seals. A scroll that was evidently similar to what was common in the Roman Empire and Jewish history. When documents were written, such as wills, they would have been presented as scrolls, sealed with up to seven seals, sealed by witnesses testifying to the validity of its contents

God's End-Time Puzzle

and conditions by which the seals could be removed. The NKJV and the ESV translations use the word "scroll" in place of the KJV rendition of "book." In either of them, the document was sealed.

What can we learn from the Scriptures about this scroll?

1. The scroll, sealed with seven seals, could only be opened when the conditions were met. The writing on the outside of the scroll was to indicate the conditions under which a seal's removal could occur, not that the seal was opened to allow something to happen. All the seals needed to be opened to reveal the contents of the scroll.

2. Who was able to remove the seals? Evidently, according to verse one above, it was God who held the scroll. Something happened on the earth, necessitating a search to be made for someone having the right to remove the seal from the scroll.

3. It is the "Lion of the tribe of Judah" who has the right to open or remove the seals. However, it was Jesus, *the Lamb of God*, who opened the seals, proving, I believe, that salvation was still available while opening these seals. Once all seven of the seals were removed, God's wrath would be revealed.

4. The scroll reveals to us its contents. When fully opened, the scroll would reveal the wrath of God that would be administered by Jesus as the "Lion of the tribe of Judah." The judgments must occur for Jesus to reclaim the earth as God's property and for His kingdom to be set up.

The Scroll

5. But Jesus would only open the seals as the *Lamb of God*, not as "The Lion of the tribe of Judah," revealing to us that God's wrath is not poured out, as it was the Lamb who opened the seals.

Verses 2–5 indicate no one was found in heaven able to open the scroll except the "Lion of the tribe of Judah." This term, "Lion of the tribe of Judah," is a term used for Jesus when He pours out His wrath upon planet Earth during the end-time. However, it is not the "Lion" who opens the scroll; it is the "Lamb" (verse 6). Jesus the Lamb—"Behold the Lamb of God, who takes away the sin of the world!" (John 1:29)—will open the scroll.

When the Lamb takes the scroll to open it, Scripture tells us that at this point, salvation will still be available to all who call upon the name of Jesus. God's wrath is not being poured out during the opening of these seals.

Now let's turn to chapter 6 of Revelation, where the seals on the scroll are opened. Along with this Revelation scripture, we will also look at the Olivet discourse as recorded in Matthew 24.

The Outside of the Scroll

The condition required for removal of the first seal had occurred. A search was made for the one who had the right and responsibility to remove it. The seal was then opened, and John was shown the reason for its removal.

Jesus, in His Olivet discourse, reveals details that correlate with the seal openings of Revelation, chapter 6.

And Jesus went out, and departed from the temple: and his disciples came to him for to shew him the buildings of the temple. And Jesus said unto them, See ye not all these things? verily I say unto you, There shall not be left here one stone upon another, that shall not be thrown down. And as he sat upon the mount of Olives, the disciples came unto him privately, saying, Tell us, when shall these things be? and what shall be the sign of thy coming, and of the end of the world? And Jesus answered and said unto them, Take heed that no man deceive you. For many shall come in my name, saying, I am Christ; and shall deceive many.

Matthew 24:1–5 (KJV)

Who Removed the Seals?

- I believe it was Jesus, the "Lion of the tribe of Judah," who was the one who wrote the scroll.
- It is evident that the scroll, when fully opened, would reveal its contents: the "wrath of God."
- Requirements for removal of the seals were that certain conditions had first to be met.
- Jesus, as the "Lion of the tribe of Judah," was the one found responsible for the removal of the seals.
- However, the Lion turned over the seals' removal to Jesus the Lamb, so salvation would be available during the perilous times following their removal.

The Scroll

Points to Ponder

1. Who sealed the scroll?
2. Who removes the seal from the scroll?
3. What causes the seal to be removed?
4. What does it mean that the "Lion of the tribe of Judah" has the right to remove the seals?
5. What does it mean that it was the Lamb who removed the seals?
6. What does the scroll reveal when fully opened?

22

Seal One.
The Deceiver Comes

"And Jesus answered them, 'See that no one leads you astray. For many will come in my name, saying, "I am the Christ," and they will lead many astray'" (Matthew 24:4–5).

Now I watched when the Lamb opened one of the seven seals, and I heard one of the four living creatures say with a voice like thunder, "Come!" And I looked, and behold, a white horse! And its rider had a bow, and a crown was given to him, and he came out conquering, and to conquer. [...] Blessed is the one who reads aloud the words of this prophecy, and blessed are those who hear, and who keep what is written in it, for the time is near.

Revelation 6:1–2 and 1:3

When seal one is removed, it shows a white horse with its rider having a bow as he went forth to conquer. Many believe the seal openings are the beginning of God's wrath upon mankind and are only opened after the rapture of the church. Jesus stated in verse 3 above that "the time is near." Are we then to expect that the beginning of the seal events are 2,000 years in the future from the time He spoke these words? I do not believe this represents God's wrath. Remember: it is the *Lamb* that removes the seals. The Lamb does not administer wrath; I believe it is the Lion that will administer God's wrath. I believe this rider came forth to conquer with deception and diplomacy and, through his efforts, will eventually bring forth the "not yet come" empire that will evolve into the eighth beast system of the Antichrist. He comes, presenting himself as a purveyor of truth as he rides a white horse. He has a bow and a crown representing that he has both power and authority. He comes to conquer without weapons (no arrows) but with coercion and deceit. I believe that Satan disguised as Gabriel sent by God to teach him the truth. Satan recognized that Christianity was flourishing, and if left unchallenged, he (Satan) would then be unable to defeat God. He began appearing to Muhammad in 610 CE, who, at first, thought these visions were coming from evil spirits. After three years, he was instructed to warn the world about false gods and to spread the message he had received. In 613 CE, he began to preach and teach that "God is one, and He doesn't need a son." He was proclaiming with that statement that Christianity was a false religion. To soften the impact of that statement, he

Seal One. The Deceiver Comes

proclaimed that Jesus was a prophet that would return in the end-time to cleanse the world of evil and convert all people to Islam. Jesus warned us to "be not deceived." Muhammad came with deception and coercion. His religion, known as Islam, became the motivation and force behind the evolvement of the Ottoman Empire. I believe that seal one was removed from the scroll when Muhammad began his quest to deceive the people.

At this point, any wrath perceived originates from this system, not God. The "not yet come" system of Revelation 17:10–11 is discussed in chapters 11 and 12 and is shown to be a religious system that will bring forth the eighth beast empire of the Antichrist.

Points to Ponder
1. Who removes seal one—the Lion or the Lamb?
2. Why was the seal removed?
3. When is/was the seal removed?

23

Seal Two.
Wars and Rumors of War

> *"And you will hear of wars and rumors of wars. See that you are not alarmed, for this must take place, but the end is not yet"* (Matthew 24:6).

> *When he opened the second seal, I heard the second living creature say, "Come!" And out came another horse, bright red. Its rider was permitted to take peace from the Earth, so that people should slay one another, and he was given a great sword.*
> **Revelation 6:3–4**

When the red horse appears and takes peace from the earth, it will cause the removal of the second seal from the scroll. The evidence the red horse has arrived is when men begin to kill men, women, and children indiscriminately. The Islamic terrorist groups seem to be fulfilling this requirement. Is this evidence of the second seal's removal? I believe it is, but you be the judge.

Point to Ponder

What causes the seal to be removed?

24
Seal Three. Famine

"For nation will rise against nation, and kingdom against kingdom, and there will be famines and earthquakes in various places. All these are but the beginning of the birth pains" (Matthew 24:7).

When he opened the third seal, I heard the third living creature say, "Come!" And I looked, and behold, a black horse! And its rider had a pair of scales in his hand. And I heard what seemed to be a voice in the midst of the four living creatures, saying, "A quart of wheat for a denarius, and three quarts of barley for a denarius, and do not harm the oil and wine!"

Revelation 6:5–6

Still no sign of God's wrath!

The black horse appears when inflation and economic chaos arrive to make their debut upon the earth. "A quart of wheat for a denarius." It is believed that a denarius was a day's wages; therefore, a day's wages were barely enough to keep one person alive. It appears there will be a great separation between those that have and those that have not. Are we there yet? You decide if the third seal has been or is about to be removed from the scroll!

It is possible that the signing of a covenant could occur at some point during this third seal. I do believe a covenant will be signed no later than when the fourth seal is removed. Three and one-half years following this signing, the Antichrist will reveal himself by declaring himself to be God as he sets up an *abomination of desolation* at the temple site in Jerusalem. This is discussed in greater detail in the next chapter.

Points to Ponder
1. What causes seal three to be removed?
2. Why do a day's wages buy so little?

25

The Middle of the Week

Beginning of the second half of the seventieth week. See also Daniel 9:27.

The Great Tribulation

Even though verses 9–14 of Matthew 24 relate to events beginning at the midpoint of this last week, the midpoint actually begins with the *abomination of desolation*, spoken of in Matthew 24:15: "So when *you* see the *abomination of desolation* spoken of by the prophet Daniel, standing in the holy place (*let the reader understand*)."

Who is the one who will read this? It is not the Jews, for they have not yet accepted Christ as their Messiah, nor is it the unbelievers. It is you, His church. He wants you to understand what is occurring. The rapture of the church has not yet taken place. He wants you to be prepared for the evil and wickedness that will be coming upon the world through Satan's efforts.

See also Matthew 24:21 and Revelation 7:14.

Jesus is referring to Daniel's prophecy concerning the *abomination of desolation* as occurring at the midpoint of the last week of his prophecy. It is the middle of the last week of Daniel's prophecy that begins the Great Tribulation. He also states that the city and sanctuary are to be destroyed, which suggests that the sanctuary must still be in existence. It is most likely built as part of an agreement in the covenant that begins the last week of Daniel's prophecy.

Before continuing with the fourth through seventh seal openings, we must explore events occurring near the middle of this last week of Daniel's prophecy.

The Antichrist and his kingdom make a seven-year covenant with Israel. This covenant signals the beginning of Israel's final week of God's dealings with Israel.

It appears from the few scriptures I can find that the covenant will be signed by the Antichrist, his beast kingdom, and Israel. This covenant appears to bring peace to Israel for the first three and one-half years. And then Ezekiel 38:7–12 tells us:

> *Be ready and keep ready, you and all your hosts that are assembled about you, and be a guard for them. After many days you will be mustered. In the latter years you will go against the land that is restored from war, the land whose people were gathered from many peoples upon the mountains of Israel, which had been a continual waste. Its people*

The Middle of the Week

were brought out from the peoples and now dwell securely, all of them. You will advance, coming on like a storm. You will be like a cloud covering the land, you and all your hordes, and many peoples with you. "Thus says the Lord GOD: On that day, thoughts will come into your mind, and you will devise an evil scheme and say, 'I will go up against the land of unwalled villages. I will fall upon the quiet people who dwell securely, all of them dwelling without walls, and having no bars or gates,' to seize spoil and carry off plunder, to turn your hand against the waste places that are now inhabited, and the people who were gathered from the nations, who have acquired livestock and goods, who dwell at the center of the Earth."

Several events occur following the signing of the covenant, which brings us to the "middle" of the week.

1. A temple is built (prior to or within) the covenant, allowing Israel to reestablish the evening and morning burnt sacrifices (see chapter 16).

2. Israel is invaded, breaking the "peace covenant" made between the Antichrist, his kingdom, and Israel (Revelation 12:13–14).

3. The dragon (Satan) is cast out of heaven and pursues the woman (Israel). When he is unsuccessful, he turns to pursue the Christians (Revelation 12:13).

4. The dragon gives the beast (Antichrist) his power, throne, and authority (Revelation 13:2).

5. The false prophet is revealed (Revelation 13:11–13).

6. The Antichrist has the false prophet set up the "abomination of desolation" on a wing of the temple where he declares himself to be God (Revelation 13:14).

7. Two witnesses appear. "And I will grant authority to my two witnesses, and they will prophesy for 1,260 days, clothed in sackcloth" (the last half of the week) (Revelation 11:3).

Some of these events may occur earlier than the middle of the week but only come to light as part of the Great Tribulation beginning in the middle of the week. It is my understanding that the "abomination of desolation" will be when the Antichrist proclaims he is God and the image or statue is set up at the temple. From this point forward, he is only given 1,260 days till his end.

Points to Ponder
1. What is the Great Tribulation?
2. When does it occur?
3. Where does it occur?
4. Who causes the Great Tribulation?

Israel Is Invaded

> *And after the sixty-two weeks, an anointed one shall be cut off and shall have nothing. And the people of the prince who is to come shall destroy the city and the sanctuary. Its end shall come with a flood, and to the end there shall be war. Desolations are decreed. And he shall make a strong covenant with many for one week, and for half of the week he shall put an end to sacrifice and offering. And on the wing of abominations shall come one who makes desolate, until the decreed end is poured out on the desolator.*
>
> **Daniel 9:26–27**

The abomination of desolation spoken of by Jesus in Matthew 24:15 will occur during this last week of Daniel's prophecy and mirror the shadow of the abomination perpetrated by Antiochus Epiphanes in 167 BCE when he sacrificed a pig upon Israel's temple altar. This will occur when the Antichrist marches into Jerusalem, declaring that he is God. What activities accompany this declaration, we do not know. It may be the setting up of a statue of the Antichrist and demanding that it be worshipped. The false prophet is heavily involved in these activities, as will be seen later.

Verse 26 above states, "And the people of the prince who is to come shall destroy the city and the sanctuary." These people are subjects controlled by the Antichrist. However, it is not the Antichrist who marches in to do the destruction. It is one of his generals, probably acting on his own, who invades Israel. I would suggest that this general is none other than Gog, the chief prince of Meshach and Tubal. He attacks Israel while they are living securely in the land. He will occupy Israel until he is defeated in the battle of Armageddon.

The only information we have about Gog is found in the Old Testament (Ezekiel, chapters 38 and 39). The reference to Gog in the book of Revelation concerns a time after the millennial reign of Christ; it is not applicable to the study of the tribulation period.

Please read Ezekiel, chapters 38 and 39.

Ezekiel reveals to us the leader of a coalition of nations, which is invading Israel during a time of peace, is Gog of the land of Magog. He is also listed as the chief prince of Meshach and Tubal. The location of Magog is debated among biblical scholars. Some assert this land is way up in Russia, while others suggest it is farther south, in Asia Minor near Turkey. This discussion is best left to scholars to let them battle it out. The Scriptures indicate these people are from the land of the north. The nations indicated in the Scriptures are all Muslim countries. Gog and those conspiring with him are the nations or peoples from Meshach and Tubal, Persia, Cush, Put, Gomer, and Beth Togarmah (see Ezekiel 38:2, 5–6). These nations represent all or portions of Iran, Iraq, Ethiopia, Yemen, Somalia, Sudan, Libya, Egypt, North Africa, and Ukraine.

The timing of their attack on Israel seems to have many scholars puzzled. There seems to be no indication in the book of Revelation that would lead us to when this event would occur. There are hints, however, in passages in both Ezekiel and Revelation that may lead us to an answer. First, Ezekiel 38:8 says:

> *After many days you will be mustered. In the latter years you will go against the land that is restored from war, the land whose people were gathered from many peoples upon the mountains of Israel, which had been a continual waste. Its people were brought out from the peoples and now dwell securely, all of them.*

Israel has been gathered from many nations, but they sure do not live in safety. When is this going to happen? Evidently, there will be a time of peace for Israel lasting for just under three and one-half years, in the first half of the seven-year covenant that begins the last week of Daniel's prophesy. There are also clues presented in both Ezekiel's prophecy and that of John's.

> *But on that day, the day that Gog shall come against the land of Israel, declares the Lord God, my wrath will be roused in my anger. For in my jealousy and in my blazing wrath I declare, On that day there shall be a great Earthquake in the land of Israel.*
> **Ezekiel 38:18–19**

God declares that an earthquake will occur in the land of Israel. It will happen in the middle of the week when Gog attacks Israel. It is most likely a local earthquake, whereas the earthquake of the sixth seal appears to be of a much larger scale.

Revelation 6:12–14 reveals an earthquake as a result of the sixth seal's removal. This earthquake would occur later after the activities of the Antichrist and his false prophet when Jesus cuts short the Great Tribulation.

> *When he opened the sixth seal, I looked, and behold, there was a great Earthquake, and the sun became black as sackcloth, the full moon became like blood, and the stars of the sky fell to the Earth as the fig tree sheds its winter fruit when shaken by a gale. The sky vanished like a scroll that is being rolled up, and every mountain and island was removed from its place. Then I saw an angel standing in the sun, and with a loud voice he called to all the birds that fly directly overhead, "Come, gather for the great supper of God, to eat the flesh of kings, the flesh of captains, the flesh of mighty men, the flesh of horses and their riders, and the flesh of all men, both free and slave, both small and great."*
>
> **Revelation 19:17–18**

Ezekiel 39:4, 17–19 says of Gog,

> *You shall fall on the mountains of Israel, you and all your hordes and the peoples who are with you. I will give you to birds of prey of every sort and to the Beasts of the field to be devoured. [...] As for you, son of man, thus says the Lord GOD: Speak to the birds*

> *of every sort and to all Beasts of the field, "Assemble and come, gather from all around to the sacrificial feast that I am preparing for you, a great sacrificial feast on the mountains of Israel, and you shall eat flesh and drink blood. You shall eat the flesh of the mighty, and drink the blood of the princes of the Earth—of rams, of lambs, and of he-goats, of bulls, all of them fat Beasts of Bashan. And you shall eat fat till you are filled, and drink blood till you are drunk, at the sacrificial feast that I am preparing for you."*

We see in these scriptures from Ezekiel and Revelation evidence that these are probably referring to the same event. If they are, then Gog is destroyed at the battle of Armageddon, as is the Antichrist, as well as the kings of the east as they all have gathered for their final confrontation with God. Some have argued that Gog is the Antichrist. This cannot be correct, as Ezekiel 39:11 reveals that Gog is buried in Israel:

> *On that day I will give to Gog a place for burial in Israel, the Valley of the Travelers, east of the sea. It will block the travelers, for there Gog and all his multitude will be buried. It will be called the Valley of Hamon-Gog.*

Revelation 19:20 declares that the beast (Antichrist) and the false prophet are thrown alive into the lake of fire.

> *And the Beast was captured, and with it the false prophet who in its presence had done*

the signs by which he deceived those who had received the mark of the Beast and those who worshiped its image. These two were thrown alive into the lake of fire that burns with sulfur.

As to exactly when God responds to the activities of the Antichrist and Gog, we do not know. We do know, however, that He will respond at some point following Gog's attack on Israel. His response will begin with an earthquake followed by signs that God's wrath is about to be poured out, as revealed when John describes it when the sixth seal has been removed from the scroll (Revelation 6:12).

His response following the signs will be:

- The angel will fly throughout the world, declaring,

    Then I saw another angel flying directly overhead, with an eternal gospel to proclaim to those who dwell on earth, to every nation and tribe and language and people. And he said with a loud voice, "Fear God and give him glory, because the hour of his judgment has come, and worship him who made heaven and earth, the sea and the springs of water."
    Revelation 14:6–7

- The church will be raptured (Revelation 7:9–17; 14:14–16).
- The 144,000 Jews will be sealed (Revelation 7:1–8).
- God's wrath will be poured out (Revelation 14:17–20).

The Middle of the Week

Points to Ponder
1. Who invades Israel?
2. Why does he invade Israel?
3. When does he invade?

The Woman and the Dragon

This event appears to occur in the middle of the week and is likely to be part of the invasion from Gog in a time of peace.

Now we have another interlude where John gets more information concerning the events of Daniel's last-week prophecy. John has just recorded the last of the trumpet soundings. Now the focus turns to an event that took place at the beginning of the birth of Israel. We see a great drama occurring where Satan is trying to squash the efforts of God to complete His plan of bringing salvation to the whole world. Satan, of course, has been busy from the moment of creation in his efforts to destroy God's plan.

Here, we see an extremely short summary of events when Jesus Christ was about to be born.

Genesis 1:14 (KJV) tells us there will be signs appearing in heaven, "And God said, Let there be lights in the firmament of the heaven to divide the day from the night; and *let them be for signs*, and for seasons, and for days, and years." What was this sign? It was most likely the symbolic story written in the stars.

John recorded what he saw, represented by the sun, moon, and stars. The wise men who came to Jerusalem, searching for Jesus, explained that they had seen His star in the east. Jesus in Luke 21:25 said, "And there will be signs in the sun and moon and stars," so celestial signs are appropriate for showing what is about to happen.

The Middle of the Week

And a great sign appeared in heaven: a woman clothed with the sun, with the moon under her feet, and on her head a crown of twelve stars. She was pregnant and was crying out in birth pains and the agony of giving birth. And another sign appeared in heaven: behold, a great red dragon, with seven heads and ten horns, and on his heads seven diadems. His tail swept down a third of the stars of heaven and cast them to the Earth. And the dragon stood before the woman who was about to give birth, so that when she bore her child he might devour it. She gave birth to a male child, one who is to rule all the nations with a rod of iron, but her child was caught up to God and to his throne.

Revelation 12:1–5

The "she" mentioned in verses 2 and 5 is symbolic of the nation of Israel about to give birth to Jesus Christ, the Son of God. Another sign appearing is Satan, pictured here as "an enormous red dragon with seven heads and ten horns and seven crowns on his heads" (verse 3, NIV). His intention, of course, was to *devour* her child the moment He was born (verse 4). Jesus was born, and God protected Him until He finished His work and went to heaven, where He now sits at the right hand of the Father.

Joseph had a similar dream long before Israel ever became a nation. That dream gives us a clue as to the meaning of John's vision (see Genesis 37:9).

Here we have correlating scriptures helping us define the symbolism John records.

Daniel 7:23–26 tells us,

> *Thus he said: "As for the fourth Beast, there shall be a fourth Kingdom on Earth, which shall be different from all the Kingdoms, and it shall devour the whole Earth, and trample it down, and break it to pieces. As for the ten horns, out of this Kingdom ten kings shall arise, and another shall arise after them; he shall be different from the former ones, and shall put down three kings. He shall speak words against the Most High, and shall wear out the saints of the Most High, and shall think to change the times and the law; and they shall be given into his hand for a time, times, and half a time. But the court shall sit in judgment, and his dominion shall be taken away, to be consumed and destroyed to the end."*

Daniel says this fourth beast will be different. What makes this kingdom any different from the other kingdoms before it? This kingdom is different in that Satan originates it as a "spiritual kingdom" with himself as its god. This kingdom is a coalition of political nations uniting with the Antichrist. I believe he rules these nations from a spiritual aspect, namely Islam. Islam has a goal to rule the world and abolish the Jews and Christians and all they stand for. This kingdom will be at the height of its power during this end-time. The Antichrist will emerge from somewhere in the Middle East once ruled by the Seleucid division of the Grecian Empire. He will form a ten-nation confederacy and will have such power and authority through being a leader of Islam that he will subdue three of its kings, most likely through their reluctance to go along with him. He will emerge with absolute authority to do as he pleases. It is evident at this point the Antichrist will begin to make his move concerning his goal: to annihilate the Christians and Jews. He will start with his plan to annihilate the Jews.

Now the scene moves forward to the time of Daniel's seventieth week, to the middle of the week, to be precise.

> *And the woman fled into the wilderness, where she has a place prepared by God, in which she is to be nourished for 1,260 days. Now war arose in heaven, Michael and his angels fighting against the dragon. And the dragon and his angels fought back, but he was defeated and there was no longer any place for them in heaven. And the great dragon was thrown down, that ancient serpent, who is called the devil and Satan, the deceiver of the whole world—he was thrown down to the Earth, and his angels were thrown down with him.*
>
> **Revelation 12:6–9**

John, now brought back from what he saw, hears a voice. What he saw was a symbolic vision of the efforts of Satan to defeat the plan of God. He is told what will happen after Satan is cast out of heaven. From this point on, this portion of Scripture occurs at the midpoint of the end-time. It is when Satan possesses the Antichrist. Now Satan is in control of this ten-nation confederacy through the person of the Antichrist.

And I heard a loud voice in heaven, saying, "Now the salvation and the power and the Kingdom of our God and the authority of his Christ have come, for the accuser of our brothers has been thrown down, who accuses them day and night before our God. And they have conquered him by the blood of the Lamb and by the word of their testimony, for they loved not their lives even unto death. Therefore, rejoice, O heavens and you who dwell in them! But woe to you, O Earth and sea, for the devil has come down to you in great wrath, because he knows that his time is short!" And when the dragon saw that he had been thrown down to the Earth, he pursued the woman who had given birth to the male child. But the woman was given the two wings of the great eagle so that she might fly from the serpent into the wilderness, to the place where she is to be nourished for a time, and times, and half a time. The serpent poured water like a river out of his mouth after the woman, to sweep her away with a flood. But the Earth came to the help of the woman, and the Earth opened its mouth and swallowed the river that the dragon had poured from his mouth. Then the dragon became furious with the woman and went off to make war on the rest of her offspring, on those who keep the commandments of God and hold to the testimony of Jesus. And he stood on the sand of the sea. And I saw a Beast rising out of the sea, with ten horns and seven heads, with

ten diadems on its horns and blasphemous names on its heads.
Revelation 12:10–13:1

It is Michael, the restrainer, who casts Satan out of heaven and defeats him. Let us look to see what other scriptures have to say concerning this.

Daniel 12:1 (KJV) tells us,

> *And at that time shall Michael stand up, the great prince which standeth for the children of thy people: and there shall be a time of trouble, such as never was since there was a nation even to that same time: and at that time thy people shall be delivered, every one that shall be found written in the book.*

Michael, the restrainer, described as the protector of God's people, has cast Satan out of heaven where he can no longer accuse the saints before God.

Note: Daniel places this event in the middle of the week when he uses the term "there shall be a time of trouble," a reference to Jeremiah's prophecy in Jeremiah 30:7: "Alas! That day is so great there is none like it; it is a time of distress for Jacob; yet he shall be saved out of it."

> *And he shall make a strong covenant with many for one week, and for half of the week he shall put an end to sacrifice and offering. And on the wing of abominations shall come one who makes desolate, until the decreed end is poured out on the desolator.*
> **Daniel 9:27**

Michael could also be the one referred to in 2 Thessalonians 2:5–8 (NIV):

> *Don't you remember that when I was with you I used to tell you these things? And now you know what is holding him back, so that he may be revealed at the proper time. For the secret power of lawlessness is already at work; but the one who now holds it back will continue to do so till he is taken out of the way. And then the lawless one will be revealed, whom the Lord Jesus will overthrow with the breath of his mouth and destroy by the splendor of his coming.*

Paul tells us the restrainer "is taken out of the way" (verse 7) so that he (the Antichrist) may be revealed at the proper time (verse 6). He refers to this restrainer as *one*, not the "church," which is a reference to many. This happens in the middle of Daniel's seventieth-week prophecy. The "middle of the week" and the rapture have not yet occurred. Paul then reveals to us that the Antichrist will only be revealed when "the one who now holds it back will continue to do so till he is taken out of the way." The Antichrist will only be revealed at the proper time (see verse 6 above). The proper time is the middle of the week when the Antichrist marches into Jerusalem, proclaiming that he is God.

Daniel 9:27 says the desolator (Antichrist) "will put an end to sacrifice and offering" in the middle of the week, which coincides with what we found in Revelation, chapter 13.

The Middle of the Week

John reveals that he saw a beast rising out of the sea, looking like a leopard with a bear's feet and with a mouth like a lion's, and that the dragon (Satan) gave his power, throne, and great authority to the beast. He then states in Revelation 13:3–5:

> *One of its heads seemed to have a mortal wound, but its mortal wound was healed, and the whole Earth marveled as they followed the Beast. And they worshiped the dragon, for he had given his authority to the Beast, and they worshiped the Beast, saying, "Who is like the Beast, and who can fight against it?" And the Beast was given a mouth uttering haughty and blasphemous words, and it was allowed to exercise authority for forty-two months.*

This beast, which is essentially the same as in Daniel's description in Daniel 7, receives power and authority from Satan himself (verse 2 above). It happens when Satan possesses the Antichrist, the absolute ruler of this ten-nation confederacy, now known as the beast, the fourth beast of Daniels's prophecy. The beast referred to is not only the Antichrist himself but also his ten-nation coalition. The makeup of this alliance was political but ruled by a religious fanatic, the Antichrist. Verse 4 reveals they worshiped the dragon. We know this dragon as Allah, the god of Islam. Satan has desired to replace God, usurp His power, and be worshipped from the very beginning of creation. Verse 3 tells us that one of the heads of this coalition, a king or ruler over one of the seven parts of this remaining coalition, seemed to have a mortal wound.

This one could be the Antichrist, who is the head of this coalition of nations. He is the one who speaks for this coalition.

> *It opened its mouth to blaspheme God, and to slander his name and his dwelling place and those who live in heaven. It was given power to wage war against God's holy people and to conquer them. And it was given authority over every tribe, people, language and nation. All inhabitants of the Earth will worship the Beast—all whose names have not been written in the Lamb's book of life, the Lamb who was slain from the creation of the world. Whoever has ears, let them hear. "If anyone is to go into captivity, into captivity they will go. If anyone is to be killed with the sword, with the sword they will be killed." This calls for patient endurance and faithfulness on the part of God's people.*
> **Revelation 13:6–10 (NIV)**

Notice: the Antichrist is given authority over "every tribe, people, language and nation" on this planet. We can now understand this Antichrist will be accepted worldwide by the Islamic community as their supreme spiritual authority: even *all who dwell on the earth will worship him* except the ones who have their names written in the book of life. They will do his bidding in his attempt to rid the world of Christians and Jews. Just how extensive their destruction will be remains to be seen.

The Middle of the Week

When the Muslims realize the Islamic Christ, the Mahdi (the Antichrist from the Christian perspective) has arrived. They (Muslims) will be obedient to Mahdi's desires. Jihad against the Christians and Jews will intensify a hundredfold even in non-Muslim nations. Political powers will seem to be powerless to stop them.

The evidence, I believe, can be seen today:

- Where else is there an enemy that hates the Jew and Christian as we see in the religion of Islam?
- Who else has the desire to rule the world like Islam?
- What is their motive now? Is it not to totally wipe out Israel and, along with them, the Christians?

The evidence is clear: this is a religious coalition, and that is why it is different from other kingdoms. This coalition is a political system of nations ruled religiously by an imam or caliphate of Islam. Islam is spreading worldwide and has adherents in virtually every nation on this globe. Islam teaches that it is permissible and right to kill infidels. Infidels, according to Islam, are those who do not accept Islam. Therefore, they think that by killing Christians and Jews, they are doing their god (Allah) a service. And that by doing so, they will have automatic admittance into heaven with seventy-two virgins. It is no wonder that, even now, they are willing to commit suicide to kill infidels.

Points to Ponder

1. Who or what is the dragon?
2. What is the dragon's motive?
3. What does the dragon do?

The Middle of the Week

The Dragon Gives the Beast His Authority

> *"And the beast that I saw was like a leopard; its feet were like a bear's, and its mouth was like a lion's mouth. And to it the dragon gave his power and his throne and great authority" (Revelation 13:2).*

It will be at this time when Israel will understand their covenant with the Antichrist and his kingdom was a covenant with death because his general, Gog, will have invaded Jerusalem. I believe the Satan-possessed Antichrist will come into Jerusalem under the cloak of "protector of the covenant." The false prophet will then set up the abomination spoken of by Daniel the Prophet on the temple site; the Antichrist will then come in, making a proclamation that he is God (see Isaiah 25:15–18).

This is the same covenant Daniel prophesied about in Daniel 9:27.

Points to Ponder

1. Who did the dragon give "his power, and his throne and great authority"?
2. How did he give him his authority?

The False Prophet

> *Then I saw another Beast rising out of the Earth. It had two horns like a lamb and it spoke like a dragon. It exercises all the authority of the first Beast in its presence, and makes the Earth and its inhabitants worship the first Beast, whose mortal wound was healed. It performs great signs, even making fire come down from heaven to Earth in front of people, and by the signs that it is allowed to work in the presence of the Beast it deceives those who dwell on Earth, telling them to make an image for the Beast that was wounded by the sword and yet lived. And it was allowed to give breath to the image of the Beast, so that the image of the Beast might even speak and might cause those who would not worship the image of the Beast to be slain. Also it causes all, both small and great, both rich and poor, both free and slave, to be marked on the right hand or the forehead, so that no one can buy or sell unless he has the mark, that is, the name of the Beast or the number of its name. This calls for wisdom: let the one who has understanding calculate the number of the Beast, for it is the number of a man, and his number is 666.*
>
> **Revelation 13:11–18**

Several things need to be understood concerning this second beast rising out of the earth with *two horns like a lamb*.

The Middle of the Week

The first thing we need to note is that this is the only information we have concerning this beast, with only one other isolated reference in Revelation 19:20:

> *And the Beast was captured, and with it the false prophet who in its presence had done the signs by which he deceived those who had received the mark of the Beast and those who worshiped its image. These two were thrown alive into the lake of fire that burns with sulfur.*

And also a reference in Matthew 24:24: "For false christs and false prophets will arise and perform great signs and wonders, so as to lead astray, *if possible, even the elect.*"

Jesus here declares that false prophets will arise, some with the power to perform signs and wonders. However, verses 12 and 14 of Revelation 13 and verse 20 of Revelation 19 seem to indicate the false prophet's power to do his miracles *is only while he is in the presence of the Antichrist, who was given satanic power.* It seems evident here the power of the false prophet is diminished while not in the presence of the Antichrist, who is possessed by Satan. Satan was not omnipresent, nor can his power be used without his presence.

Next, we need to understand that the "beast" references throughout the Bible always refer to either a kingdom or the ruler of that kingdom. This "beast" should be looked at with the same understanding. Both the ruler and a kingdom are in view. Therefore, we must also look at this with the same lens. The focus, however, seems to be on this "beast" as an extremely wicked individual who, with fake miracles, deceives the masses.

The *two horns like a lamb*, we then realize, are two nations rising out of the earth. They will be united under this false prophet with a singular purpose to support the efforts of the beast or the Antichrist and his kingdom. This false prophet will be the spiritual leader of these two nations.

We understand these individuals, the Antichrist and the false prophet, from the biblical perspective, to be spiritual leaders of Islam. The Bible's Antichrist, recognized by the Islamic community as the "Mahdi," their Messiah. And the Bible's false prophet is recognized as "Isa" by the Islamic community. According to Islam, this "Isa" is the biblical Jesus who will descend during the end-time for the purpose of bringing the world into Islam. He (Isa) will attempt to destroy all religions in his quest to help cleanse the world of unbelievers, including Christians and Jews, as Islam views Jesus as the Islamic prophet Isa. He (Isa) will fight for Islam and the Antichrist until the world comes to Islam and worships Allah.

Some scholars believe the false prophet rises from among the Jewish people, claiming "out of the Earth" refers to Israel. But "out of the Earth" could mean from anywhere on the earth. He is also a deceiver; he may have presented himself as a Christian or a Jew during his lifetime. Being an extremely charismatic individual, he will use his charm and deceit in an attempt to sway

The Middle of the Week

Christians and Jews into believing the lie. Remember what Jesus said in Matthew 24:24 above.

It seems by the implication of this verse that many of the false prophet's "great signs and wonders" are performed for the purpose of deceiving Christians and Jews. It is possible he may have had a close relationship with the Christian community. In addition, Revelation 13:11 suggests that he appears to be harmless as he comes in *like a lamb* but speaks *like a dragon* (with venom): "Then I saw another Beast rising out of the Earth. It had two horns like a lamb and it spoke like a dragon."

The Muslims would describe their awaited Islamic Mahdi this way:

- He is Islam's long-awaited savior.
- He is the one sought for throughout history.
- He is what Islam has dreamed for.
- He is the world's hope for salvation.
- The Mahdi will be a universal figure.

Muslims, recognizing the Mahdi will be accepted the world over by the Muslim community, will be more than willing to pledge their support and accept the "mark" (discussed later), dooming themselves to everlasting punishment in hell. (To the Christians, the Mahdi is the Antichrist.)

At this point, we need to clarify the understanding of the Antichrist and the false prophet. The Antichrist, who Christians believe will come and exert his evil ambitions, even to the point of proclaiming himself to be God at the midpoint of this last week of Daniel's prophecy, is the Mahdi of Islam. The Islamic community believes this Mahdi is their Messiah who has come to cleanse the earth of evil and bring it to a point where the whole world is worshipping Allah. Remember: Islam preaches Christians and Jews are infidels and, therefore, are evil.

The person Christians believe to be the false prophet is the same one Islam believes is Jesus who has returned to do the Mahdi's bidding. His name in Islam is Isa. When this is understood thoroughly, we see how easy it will be used for the deception of many people.

The Christians realize the Antichrist will come first, indwelt by Satan. He will have only three and one-half years from the time he proclaims himself to be God. Muslims, on the other hand, understand from their Qur'an that the Mahdi, their Messiah, will come first with the task of converting the world to Islam, which is the worship of Allah (Satan).

With this, we understand the difference between Christians and Muslims. We begin to understand why it will be easy for the Muslims to fall in line with the wishes of the Mahdi (Antichrist) to rid the world of Christians and Jews. With this, we understand jihad will reign supreme.

The false prophet, with the Mahdi's approval, will be the one overseeing the establishment of a mark that will identify the followers of the Mahdi (the Antichrist possessed by Satan). This mark will have only one purpose. It will only be for the purpose of coercing "unbelievers" to accept the mark to buy and sell. By accepting the mark, they will be sealed forever as a follower of the beast, the Antichrist, their eternal destination forever determined. The only real purpose of the mark is to ferret out Christians, Jews, and other unbelievers. The buying and selling rationale is there for the reason of deception.

Jesus said about the end-time, "Be not deceived." The mark will be sold to the world as a way to combat economic theft. No more someone trying to steal one's wealth or identity; it will be controlled by the mark on the forehead or right hand. They do not say accepting the mark identifies the recipient as a follower of Allah, but that is exactly what it does.

The false prophet presents this mark as a benign necessity for the purpose of eliminating evil.

Many books have been written proclaiming this or that about the 666 mark; let's look at what the Bible says in Revelation 13:18: "This calls for wisdom: let the one who has understanding calculate the number of the Beast, *for it is the number of a man, and his number is 666.*"

In Greek, 666 is *chixistigma*; the Greek word for man is *anthropos*, which carries with it the idea of a certain man. *We can then see this is an identifying mark of man and all that he represents.* The Antichrist is a man possessed by Satan, and this mark identifies him. Along with the mark will be information identifying the recipient as a follower of the Antichrist who is possessed by Satan.

The first thing to consider is the mark of the beast represents a kingdom, a spiritual kingdom, the kingdom of Islam, and its ruler, the Antichrist.

As we have noted in our study of the ten-nation coalition, the beast kingdom of the end-time is an Islamic coalition, a spiritual coalition. Remember Daniel said this coalition would be different. The difference is that it is not only a political coalition but also a spiritual one.

The mark associates one with the Mahdi, the Islamic Messiah, but from the Christian perspective—the Antichrist.

Several things have been presented as the "mark." Without elaboration, here are a few of the possibilities.

- The mark is the actual number 666 that will be branded or tattooed upon the right hand or the forehead.
- Barcodes, commonly used for products to scan for price and inventory information, have 666 embedded within them. They have been presented as the mark of the beast.
- A chip called the VeriChip has been offered as the mark of the beast. This chip can be inserted under the skin of the hand or forehead and will carry every bit of one's information.
- Another possibility presented is called "smart skin," a membrane-like film permanently fixed to the skin that carries all of one's information.
- Another possibility is the *Bismillah*, a headband or armband that is worn. The only problem with this is it can be taken off. Its Arabic meaning is "in the name of God," "most gracious," "most compassionate." Some interpret it to say, "In the name of Allah."[1]

[1] Wikipedia, s.v. "Basmala," last modified March 19, 2022, https://en.wikipedia.org/wiki/Basmala.

The Middle of the Week

- My feelings concerning the mark are:
- It originates in the Islamic countries of the Middle East by the beast kingdom and its false prophet.
- The Islamic countries are all nearly 100 percent Muslim.
- The mark signifies the worship of Allah.
- It will almost certainly be a visible mark where all can identify its recipient as a worshipper of Allah.
- The mark will be permanent: once taken, it will doom the recipient to hell.

Another thing the false prophet will make for the purpose of ferreting out unbelievers is an image of the beast.

> *[...] telling them to make an image for the Beast that was wounded by the sword and yet lived. And it was allowed to give breath to the image of the Beast, so that the image of the Beast might even speak and might cause those who would not worship the image of the Beast to be slain.*
> **Revelation 13:14b–15**

The false prophet will make himself known following the revealing of the Antichrist at the midpoint of the seventh week of Daniel's prophecy. It appears he may be a ruler of two Muslim nations. It seems, according to Scripture, his duties will be to point to the Antichrist as the savior of mankind and to authorize destruction to those who refuse to worship him as a god.

Points to Ponder
1. What is the makeup of the false prophet?
2. What will he do?
3. What seems to be his purpose?

The Middle of the Week

The Abomination of Desolation

> *Forces from him shall appear and profane the temple and fortress, and shall take away the regular burnt offering. And they shall set up the abomination that makes desolate. He shall seduce with flattery those who violate the covenant, but the people who know their God shall stand firm and take action. And the wise among the people shall make many understand, though for some days they shall stumble by sword and flame, by captivity and plunder. When they stumble, they shall receive a little help. And many shall join themselves to them with flattery, and some of the wise shall stumble, so that they may be refined, purified, and made white, until the time of the end, for it still awaits the appointed time. And the king shall do as he wills. He shall exalt himself and magnify himself above every god, and shall speak astonishing things against the God of gods. He shall prosper till the indignation is accomplished; for what is decreed shall be done.*
>
> **Daniel 11:31–36**

Many believe this prophecy from Daniel has already been fulfilled by Antiochus Epiphanes. Indeed, he did these things in 167 BCE. However, it is nothing more than a shadow of the end-time, as Jesus referred to this exact prophecy of Daniel as occurring in the end-time.

And deceiveth them that dwell on the Earth by the means of those miracles which he had power to do in the sight of the Beast; saying to them that dwell on the Earth, that they should make an image to the Beast, which had the wound by a sword, and did live. And he had power to give life unto the image of the Beast, that the image of the Beast should both speak, and cause that as many as would not worship the image of the Beast should be killed. And he causeth all, both small and great, rich and poor, free and bond, to receive a mark in their right hand or the forehead, And that no man might buy or sell, save he that had the mark, or the name of the Beast, or the number of his name. Here is wisdom. Let him that hath understanding count the number of the Beast: for it is the number of a man; and his number is Six hundred threescore and six.

Revelation 13:14–18 (KJV)

So when you [believers] see the abomination of desolation spoken of by the prophet Daniel, standing in the holy place (let the reader understand), then let those who are in Judea flee to the mountains. Let the one who is on the housetop not go down to take what is in his house, and let the one who is in the field not turn back to take his cloak. And alas for women who are pregnant and for those who are nursing infants in those days! Pray that your flight may not be in winter or on a Sabbath. For then there will be great tribulation, such as has not been from the beginning of the world until now, no, and never will be. And if those days had not been cut short, no human being would be saved. But for the sake of the elect those days will be cut short.

Matthew 24:15–22

We notice in the dialog that Jesus is addressing believers, those who want to know what the future holds. He is telling them that a Great Tribulation will come upon the people. This "abomination of desolation" He speaks of, as prophesied by Daniel, will be a warning to the people in Judea to flee (see also Revelation 12:6). He then says in verse 22, "And if those days had not been cut short, no human being would be saved." Jesus will cut short the Great Tribulation for the elects' (believers') sake. The rapture will occur sometime during these last three and one-half years. The word "elect" in the New Testament *always* refers to believers in Christ, not to unrepentant Jews.

The *saints* (believers in Christ) will be raptured at some point during this last three-and one-half-year period just before God's wrath. The balance of the three and one-half-year period sees God's wrath applied to all the inhabitants of the earth, except for the 144,000 sealed Jews, who, I believe, converted to Christianity at the time of the rapture. This will be explored more fully later.

Then if anyone says to you, "Look, here is the Christ!" or "There he is!" do not believe it.

For false christs and false prophets will arise and perform great signs and wonders, so as to lead astray, if possible, even the elect. See, I have told you beforehand. So, if they say to you, "Look, he is in the wilderness," do not go out. If they say, "Look, he is in the inner rooms," do not believe it. For as the lightning comes from the east and shines as far as the west, so will be the coming of the Son of Man. Wherever the corpse is, there the vultures will gather.

Matthew 24:23–28

Jesus reminds them that "false christs and false prophets" will be present during the Great Tribulation. He is referring to the Antichrist and his false prophet (the Islamic christ and his prophet). He warns them not to go out to see them and that His coming will be "as the lightning comes from the east and shines as far as the west, so will be the coming of the Son of Man."

Points to Ponder
1. What is the abomination of desolation?
2. How did the Jews react?

The Middle of the Week

The Two Witnesses

Then I was given a measuring rod like a staff, and I was told, "Rise and measure the temple of God and the altar and those who worship there, but do not measure the court outside the temple; leave that out, for it is given over to the nations, and they will trample the holy city for forty-two months. And I will grant authority to my two witnesses, and they will prophesy for 1,260 days, clothed in sackcloth." These are the two olive trees and the two lampstands that stand before the Lord of the Earth. And if anyone would harm them, fire pours from their mouth and consumes their foes. If anyone would harm them, this is how he is doomed to be killed. They have the power to shut the sky, that no rain may fall during the days of their prophesying, and they have power over the waters to turn them into blood and to strike the Earth with every kind of plague, as often as they desire. And when they have finished their testimony, the Beast that rises from the bottomless pit will make war on them and conquer them and kill them, and their dead bodies will lie in the street of the great city that symbolically is called Sodom and Egypt, where their Lord was crucified. For three and a half days some from the peoples and tribes and languages and nations will gaze at their dead bodies and refuse to let them be placed in a tomb, and those who dwell on the Earth will rejoice over them and make merry and exchange presents, because these two prophets had been a torment to those who dwell on the Earth. But after the three and a half days a breath of life from God entered them, and they stood up on their feet, and great fear fell on those who saw them. Then they heard a loud voice from heaven saying to them, "Come up here!" And they went up to heaven in a cloud, and their enemies watched them. And at that hour there was a great Earthquake, and a tenth of the city fell. Seven thousand people were killed in the Earthquake, and the rest were terrified and gave glory to the God of heaven. The second woe has passed; behold, the third woe is soon to come. Then the seventh angel blew his trumpet, and there were loud voices in heaven, saying, "The Kingdom of the world has become the Kingdom of our Lord and of his Christ, and he shall reign forever and ever."

Revelation 11:1–15

Miracles performed by the false prophet are designed to thwart the effectiveness of the two witnesses God has sent to hamper the efforts of the Antichrist and his system as they will be a thorn in their side throughout the Great Tribulation.

It is apparent these two witnesses arrive on the earth near the same time the Antichrist sets up his abomination of desolation. The Antichrist, from that moment on, is given only 1,260 days until God defeats him and sends

The Middle of the Week

him to his eternal destiny, the lake of fire. The two witnesses are given the same amount of time (forty-two months, which is also 1,260 days).

John gives more information culminating at the end of the sixth trumpet. Verse 14 says, "The second woe has passed; the third woe is coming soon."

John is told to "go and measure the temple of God and the altar, and count the worshipers there." This scripture reveals more information than meets the eye.

1. *There will be a temple standing in Jerusalem* in the middle of the seventieth week of Daniel's prophecy.

John is told not to measure the outer court, for it is given to the Gentiles who will trample on the holy city for forty-two months (1,260 days).

It reveals that the outer court, which presently houses the Dome of the Rock, will be under Gentile (Islamic) control until the end of the forty-two months.

It also reveals that this vision begins in the middle of the week but ends at the end of the sixth trumpet judgment before the seventh judgment is poured out.

2. *Power will be given to the two witnesses.*

Verse 3 above tells us that the two witnesses are given 1,260 days (forty-two months) to prophesy.

Verse 4 tells us these two witnesses "are the two olive trees and the two candlesticks that stand before the Lord of the Earth."

Zechariah 4:12–14 says,

> *And a second time I answered and said to him, "What are these two branches of the olive trees, which are beside the two golden pipes from which the golden oil is poured out?" He said to me, "Do you not know what these are?" I said, "No, my lord." Then he said, "These are the two anointed ones who stand by the Lord of the whole Earth."*

3. We do not know who these two anointed ones are.

Some scholars speculate that Moses, Elijah, Zerubbabel, or even Enoch are possible candidates for these two witnesses. We do know they have the power

> *to shut the sky, that no rain may fall during the days of their prophesying, and they have power over the waters to turn them into blood and to strike the Earth with every kind of plague, as often as they desire.*
>
> **Revelation 11:6**

On what basis are these candidates considered? Moses and Elijah were two who had great power with their miracles as they confronted the evil of their day. Enoch and Elijah—on the basis that they did not die but were taken directly into heaven. Zerubbabel—by a prophecy written by Haggai.

> *Speak to Zerubbabel, governor of Judah, saying, I am about to shake the heavens and the Earth, and to overthrow the throne of*

Kingdoms. I am about to destroy the strength of the Kingdoms of the nations, and overthrow the chariots and their riders. And the horses and their riders shall go down, every one by the sword of his brother. On that day, declares the L{small caps}ORD *of hosts, I will take you, O Zerubbabel my servant, the son of Shealtiel, declares the* L{small caps}ORD*, and make you like a signet ring, for I have chosen you, declares the* L{small caps}ORD *of hosts.*

Haggai 2:21–23

These two witnesses prophesy for 1,260 days, which corresponds to the forty-two months given the beast. They must, according to this portion of Scripture, begin their witness in the middle of Daniel's prophetic seventieth week.

When their witness has finished, the beast will overpower them and kill them. Their bodies will lie in the streets of Jerusalem for three and one-half days. The people will be so delighted they are dead that they will send gifts and rejoice at their demise. It sounds like there is great elation in the camp of the enemy that these two witnesses have been defeated, their optimism heightened as to the possibility of their victory at the upcoming battle of Armageddon. Why are these people so elated that they send gifts? Remember: this is a religious battle that has been raging between the forces of good and evil. *The church has been raptured, and salvation was not available during the period of God's wrath being poured out.* Only forces of evil have been on the earth, except for the 144,000 sealed Jews and possibly many scattered throughout the world who have not converted to Christianity and yet have not accepted the claims of Islam. The forces of evil will sense victory in their sight, with these two witnesses seemingly eliminated. The sealed Jews are now the only obstacle left, or so they will think. To the forces of evil, God will seem on the run, but He will have their plans. Optimism will be high for the wicked as the forces of evil gather some 200,000,000 troops to Armageddon to fight the forces of Good.

But God, after three and one-half days, will breathe life into the two witnesses, and the people will be terror-struck. God will call them to heaven, and calamity will fall on Jerusalem that has been trampled under the feet of the Gentiles for the last 1,260 days (three and a half years).

Revelation 11:13 says,

> *And at that hour there was a great Earthquake, and a tenth of the city fell. Seven thousand people were killed in the Earthquake, and the rest were terrified and gave glory to the God of heaven.*

The KJV states it this way:

> *And the same hour was there a great Earthquake, and the tenth part of the city fell, and in the Earthquake were slain of men seven thousand: and the remnant were affrighted, and gave glory to the God of heaven.*

The Middle of the Week

These two witnesses seem to have had their prophetic ministry centered on the seat and activity of the Antichrist, whose people had invaded Israel at the midpoint of the last week of Daniel's prophecy, trampling underfoot the holy land. The Jews had fled into hiding when the "abomination" was set up in the temple area (see Revelation 12:14–15). The "remnant," those 144,000 God had sealed, evidently had not fled into hiding but remained hidden from the Antichrist through God's sealing. The people rejoiced and sent gifts at these two witnesses' deaths but were surprised and frightened at their resurrection. That same hour God sent an earthquake, and we see the 144,000 survivors (remnant) rejoicing and giving God praise. They evidently were still dwelling in or around Jerusalem.

Verse 14 indicates to us that the second woe, which is the sixth trumpet, is over. It means these witnesses had their ministry during the time the beast was having his heyday in persecuting the Jews and the church before the rapture and also during the time God's wrath was being poured out.

If the two witnesses started their ministry at the midpoint of the week and ministered for 1,260 days to coincide with the time given to the Antichrist, then:

1. It means that the seventh week of Daniel's prophecy has been fulfilled as well as the allotted time for the Antichrist.
2. It also means the seventh trumpet has sounded, and the seventh bowl is poured out *after* the seventh week has ended.

Daniel 12:11–12 says,

> *And from the time that the regular burnt offering is taken away and the abomination that makes desolate is set up, there shall be 1,290 days. Blessed is he who waits and arrives at the 1,335 days.*

I am of the opinion that Gog will invade Jerusalem at a time of peace, thirty days before the Antichrist marches into Jerusalem to set up the abomination, causing desolation. The thirty days before the Antichrist marches into Jerusalem, starting the countdown of the 1,260 days allotted to the Antichrist, are equal to the 1,290 days mentioned in verse 11 above (see chart in chapter 16).

Could it mean that during the forty-five days following the end of the seventieth week is when the battle of Armageddon is fought, the devil is defeated, the Antichrist and false prophet are thrown into the lake of fire, and God's millennial kingdom begins?

Sometime between this event and/or as part of the seventh trumpet, the battle of Armageddon will take place, and Jesus Christ will begin to rule His kingdom.

> *Then the seventh angel blew his trumpet, and there were loud voices in heaven, saying, "The Kingdom of the world has become the Kingdom of our Lord and of his Christ, and he shall reign forever and ever."*
>
> **Revelation 11:15**

The Middle of the Week

Verse 15 also coincides with the seventh bowl judgment.

> *The seventh angel poured out his bowl into the air, and a loud voice came out of the temple, from the throne, saying, "It is done!" And there were flashes of lightning, rumblings, peals of thunder, and a great Earthquake such as there had never been since man was on the Earth, so great was that Earthquake. The great city was split into three parts, and the cities of the nations fell, and God remembered Babylon the great, to make her drain the cup of the wine of the fury of his wrath. And every island fled away, and no mountains were to be found. And great hailstones, about one hundred pounds each, fell from heaven on people; and they cursed God for the plague of the hail, because the plague was so severe.*
>
> **Revelation 16:17–21**

It appears here that Jesus was taking a massive measure to prepare the earth for His kingdom.

Points to Ponder

1. When did the two witnesses appear?
2. What seem to be their duties?
3. How long was their assignment?
4. What happened to them?

26

Seals Four and Five. Death and Martyrdom

Then they will deliver you up to tribulation and put you to death, and you will be hated by all nations for my name's sake. And then many will fall away and betray one another and hate one another. And many false prophets will arise and lead many astray. And because lawlessness will be increased, the love of many will grow cold. But the one who endures to the end will be saved. And this gospel of the Kingdom will be proclaimed throughout the whole world as a testimony to all nations, and then the end will come. So when you see the abomination of desolation spoken of by the prophet Daniel, standing in the holy place (let the reader understand).

Matthew 24:9–15

When he opened the fourth seal, I heard the voice of the fourth living creature say,

"Come!" And I looked, and behold, a pale horse! And its rider's name was Death, and Hades followed him. And they were given authority over a fourth of the Earth, to kill with sword and with famine and with pestilence and by wild Beasts of the Earth. When he opened the fifth seal; I saw under the altar the souls of those who had been slain for the word of God and for the witness they had borne. They cried out with a loud voice, "O Sovereign Lord, holy and true, how long before you will judge and avenge our blood on those who dwell on the Earth?" Then they were each given a white robe and told to rest a little longer, until the number of their fellow servants and their brothers should be complete, who were to be killed as they themselves had been.

Revelation 6:7–11

The fourth seal reveals that there must be a dire situation of people dying by "sword and with famine and with pestilence and by wild Beasts of the Earth."

The removal of the fourth seal is marked by death, famine, plague, and war. The Antichrist and his system have most likely broken their covenant with Israel, as "they were given power over a fourth of the Earth," apparently by Satan, through the Antichrist, marking the beginning of the Great Tribulation. This Antichrist will be accepted as the Islamic christ by the Muslims, believing he has come to cleanse the world of infidels and unbelievers. The power they possess seems, first of

Seals Four and Five. Death and Martyrdom

all, to be only over one-fourth of the earth, most likely the territory of the earth ruled by Islamic ideology. They will be given power to rid their territory of Christians and Jews by all available means. There are Islamist adherents in every nation on the earth, totaling more than one and one-half billion followers.

The removal of this fifth seal reveals a scene *under the altar* of all those slain because of their belief in Jesus Christ as their Redeemer, an indication the rapture has not yet taken place. The seal's removal will be because of their cry: "How long, [...] until you judge the inhabitants of the Earth and avenge our blood?" (Revelation 6:10, NIV). They will be *told to wait a little longer* because more Christians and Jews will be killed before God's wrath is poured out. I believe these Christians include all the martyrs killed because of their faith since Christianity began in the first century CE.

The fourth and fifth seal openings will most likely occur as part of the Great Tribulation beginning in the middle of the last week of Daniel's prophecy.

These Christians are seen "under the altar," evidently a holding area for the Christians who have died before the rapture. Also, they seem to understand that God's wrath has not yet been poured out. We will also see, in Revelation 7:9–17, the real picture of the rapture having taken place, as they are in the very presence of God and the angels. This event will take place after the sixth seal is removed.

Points to Ponder
1. What does it mean when you see the "abomination of desolation"?
2. What does it infer when it says, "I saw under the altar the souls of those who had been slain"?

27

Seal Six. God Announces His Coming with the Signs!

Immediately after the tribulation of those days the sun will be darkened, and the moon will not give its light, and the stars will fall from heaven, and the powers of the heavens will be shaken. Then will appear in heaven the sign of the Son of Man, and then all the tribes of the Earth will mourn, and they will see the Son of Man coming on the clouds of heaven with power and great glory. And he will send out his angels with a loud trumpet call, and they will gather his elect from the four winds, from one end of heaven to the other.

Matthew 24:29–31

When he opened the sixth seal, I looked, and behold, there was a great Earthquake, and the sun became black as sackcloth, the full moon became like blood, and the stars of the sky fell to the Earth as the fig tree sheds its winter fruit when shaken by a gale. The sky vanished like a scroll that is being rolled up, and every mountain and island was removed from its place. Then the kings of the Earth and the great ones and the generals and the rich and the powerful, and everyone, slave and free, hid themselves in the caves and among the rocks of the mountains, calling to the mountains and rocks, "Fall on us and hide us from the face of him who is seated on the throne, and from the wrath of the Lamb, for the great day of their wrath has come, and who can stand?"

Revelation 6:12–17

Jesus said, "Immediately after the tribulation." It is evident the tribulation is not a result of God's wrath, as the signs have not yet occurred. The Great Tribulation Jesus referred to in His Olivet discourse (Matthew 24:21) starts when the Antichrist sets up the *abomination of desolation* and turns his focus on the Christians and Jews (see Revelation 12:13–17). The signs marking the coming of *the Lord's day* (God's wrath) will follow the Great Tribulation brought on by the wrath of Satan through the Antichrist.

Note: Jesus said He will come "on the clouds of heaven." He will come to rapture His church, not to fight the battle of Armageddon. There is no indication here that Jesus will descend all the way to the earth. Note these words from 1 Thessalonians 4:16–17:

Seal Six. God Announces His Coming with the Signs!

> *For the Lord himself will descend from heaven with a cry of command, with the voice of an archangel, and with the sound of the trumpet of God. And the dead in Christ will rise first. Then we who are alive, who are left, will be caught up together with them in the clouds to meet the Lord in the air, and so we will always be with the Lord.*

This scripture agrees with what Jesus said in Matthew 24:29–31. Paul told us the raptured saints would meet Jesus in the air. Jesus is telling us that there will be signs before the rapture and after the tribulation and that He will meet them "in the clouds."

When the Antichrist sets up the abomination causing desolation, he has but three and one-half years to accomplish his evil plan—the last half of Daniel's seventieth-week prophecy as recorded in Daniel 9:27. This last three and one-half-year period is understood as the Great Tribulation. Jesus said in Matthew 24:22, "*If those days had not been cut short*, no human being would be saved. But for the sake of the elect those days will be cut short."

This Great Tribulation, shortened for the elects' (believers') sake, does not mean the Great Tribulation has been cut short for those left behind. Satan and his deceptive partner, the Antichrist, will still have their allotted time of three-and-one-half years. Jesus will cut short this Great Tribulation for the elects' (believers') sake by an event we call the rapture. Signs that the rapture is imminent will appear in the sky. Luke 21:28 tells us when we see these "events" (the signs), *we are to look up, for our redemption (rapture) draws nigh.* God's wrath will follow.

The Scriptures seem to tell us Satan and Antichrist will have their way during the events following the abomination of desolation, which will occur in the middle of the week. However, the tables are turned when God begins to pour out His wrath. The Old Testament prophets tell us that "the Lord alone will be exalted in that day": "The haughty looks of man shall be brought low, and the lofty pride of men shall be humbled, and *the LORD alone will be exalted in that day*" (Isaiah 2:11).

> *After this I saw four angels standing at the four corners of the Earth, holding back the four winds of the Earth, that no wind might blow on Earth or sea or against any tree. Then I saw another angel ascending from the rising of the sun, with the seal of the living God, and he called with a loud voice to the four angels who had been given power to harm Earth and sea, saying, "Do not harm the Earth or the sea or the trees, until we have sealed the servants of our God on their foreheads." And I heard the number of the sealed, 144,000, sealed from every tribe of the sons of Israel.*
>
> **Revelation 7:1–4**

> *After this I looked, and behold, a great multitude that no one could number, from every nation, from all tribes and peoples and*

Seal Six. God Announces His Coming with the Signs!

> *languages, standing before the throne and before the Lamb, clothed in white robes, with palm branches in their hands, and crying out with a loud voice, "Salvation belongs to our God who sits on the throne, and to the Lamb!" And all the angels were standing around the throne and around the elders and the four living creatures, and they fell on their faces before the throne and worshiped God saying, "Amen! Blessing and glory and wisdom and thanksgiving and honor and power and might be to our God forever and ever! Amen." Then one of the elders addressed me, saying, "Who are these, clothed in white robes, and from where have they come?" I said to him, "Sir, you know." And he said to me, "These are the ones coming out of the great tribulation. They have washed their robes and made them white in the blood of the Lamb. Therefore they are before the throne of God, and serve him day and night in his temple; and he who sits on the throne will shelter them with his presence. They shall hunger no more, neither thirst anymore; the sun shall not strike them, nor any scorching heat. For the Lamb in the midst of the throne will be their shepherd, and he will guide them to springs of living water, and God will wipe away every tear from their eyes."*
>
> **Revelation 7:9–17**

He saw four angels preparing themselves to pour out God's wrath when another angel told them to wait until

God's End-Time Puzzle

they had sealed 144,000 Jews. After the sealing, John saw an event in heaven that can only be described as *the rapture*. *All* the angels were surrounding these saints that suddenly found themselves standing in the presence of the Lamb.

The claim that the 144,000 Jews are evangelists is just an assumption. They were sealed at the same time the rapture of the church occurred. The Scriptures reveal to us that following the rapture, the temple in heaven will be closed, indicating salvation will not be available during the time of God's wrath.

In Revelation 7:1 and 7:9, we see the term "after this." John wants us to know that these two events take place *after* the signs that Jesus and the prophets said would appear *before* the beginning of the Lord's day (God's wrath).

Points to Ponder

1. Why do signs appear in heaven and on the earth?
2. Why will everyone seem to hide?

28

The Rapture and the Wrath

Then I looked, and behold, on Mount Zion stood the Lamb, and with him 144,000 who had his name and his Father's name written on their foreheads. And I heard a voice from heaven like the roar of many waters and like the sound of loud thunder. The voice I heard was like the sound of harpists playing on their harps, and they were singing a new song before the throne and before the four living creatures and before the elders. No one could learn that song except the 144,000 who had been redeemed from the Earth. It is these who have not defiled themselves with women, for they are virgins. It is these who follow the Lamb wherever he goes. These have been redeemed from mankind as firstfruits for God and the Lamb, and in their mouth no lie was found, for they are blameless.

Revelation 14:1–5

John sees in a vision 144,000 Jews sealed by the Holy Spirit following the rapture of the church but before God's wrath had begun. He sees them standing with Jesus before Mount Zion, the spiritual reference to Jerusalem. John then hears a sound from heaven, sounding "like the sound of harpists playing on their harps." Who were these that sounded like they were playing their harps?

In looking at Revelation 15:1–3, we see John looking to heaven where he hears these harpists again, and we can then begin to see the relationship between this group and those of Revelation 14:1–5.

> *Then I saw another sign in heaven, great and amazing, seven angels with seven plagues, which are the last, for with them the wrath of God is finished. And I saw what appeared to be a sea of glass mingled with fire—and those who had conquered the Beast and its image and the number of its name, standing beside the sea of glass with harps of God in their hands. And they sing the song of Moses, the servant of God, and the song of the Lamb, saying, "Great and amazing are your deeds, O Lord God the Almighty! Just and true are your ways, O King of the nations!"*

We now can conclude:
1. This event takes place before the pouring out of God's wrath (verse 1). The *seven plagues* have not yet been poured out as they were still in possession by the angels, and since they run concurrent with the trumpet judgments, we must conclude this event is indeed before God's wrath.

2. The rapture had occurred since we see the raptured church in heaven standing "beside the sea" with harps and singing "the song of Moses, the servant of God, and the song of the Lamb." They were victorious over "the Beast and its image and the number of its name." Note: both the Old Testament saints (those singing the song of Moses) and the New Testament saints (those singing the song of the Lamb) are included in this group standing beside the sea.

3. The rapture occurred after the false prophet had made the image of the Antichrist and the establishment of his mark, as the raptured here had been victorious over both before the rapture took place.

4. The song they sang was a song of redemption only the redeemed could sing.

5. This event with Jesus standing with the 144,000 on Mount Zion was symbolic, as, at this time, the Antichrist had caused the Jews to flee Jerusalem. Protection, however, was provided for 1,260 days for the 144,000 while in hiding. They fled Jerusalem at the midpoint of this last week of Daniel's prophecy but also may have returned and stayed in hiding after they were sealed. These 144,000 Jews are the remnant referred to by Paul in Romans 9:27 (NIV): "Isaiah cries out concerning Israel: 'Though the number of the Israelites be like the sand by the sea, only the remnant will be saved.'"

Are we then to understand that there will only be 144,000 Jews redeemed?

God's End-Time Puzzle

Revelation 7 gives us this picture:

1. The first six seals of the scroll have been removed.
2. The seventh seal revealing the judgments of God, which are "God's wrath," has not yet been removed.
3. As we have already shown, God's wrath is a time of judgment upon the wicked. Heaven's temple was closed, so salvation was not available during this time of wrath (you will understand this later).
4. The 144,000 were redeemed and sealed for their protection just before God's wrath was poured out.
5. The rapture had also occurred just before this time of wrath.
6. The reason the 144,000 were the only ones that could learn this song was that this event takes place immediately after the rapture, where the Old and New Testament believers were taken to heaven. The 144,000, realizing the rapture had taken place and Jesus Christ must certainly have been their Messiah, turned to God immediately after the rapture, and before God's wrath began, God then sealed them. They are pictured here as redeemed and as the firstfruits of the Jews' salvation.

Remember, events recorded in Revelation are not necessarily in sequential order. The vision was given to John as in Revelation 14:1–5 and must couple with his vision of Revelation 15:1–3.

Another scripture that can be placed at this point is Revelation 19:1–10:

The Rapture and the Wrath

After this I heard what seemed to be the loud voice of a great multitude in heaven, crying out, "Hallelujah! Salvation and glory and power belong to our God, for his judgments are true and just; for he has judged the great prostitute who corrupted the Earth with her immorality, and has avenged on her the blood of his servants." Once more they cried out, "Hallelujah! The smoke from her goes up forever and ever." And the twenty-four elders and the four living creatures fell down and worshiped God who was seated on the throne, saying, "Amen. Hallelujah!" And from the throne came a voice saying, "Praise our God, all you his servants, you who fear him, small and great." Then I heard what seemed to be the voice of a great multitude, like the roar of many waters and like the sound of mighty peals of thunder, crying out, "Hallelujah! For the Lord our God the Almighty reigns. Let us rejoice and exult and give him the glory, for the marriage of the Lamb has come, and his Bride has made herself ready; it was granted her to clothe herself with fine linen, bright and pure"— for the fine linen is the righteous deeds of the saints. *And the angel said to me, "Write this: Blessed are those who are invited to the marriage supper of the Lamb." And he said to me, "These are the true words of God." Then I fell down at his feet to worship him, but he said to me, "You must not do that! I am a fellow servant with you and your brothers who hold to the testimony of Jesus. Worship*

God." For the testimony of Jesus is the spirit of prophecy.

This scripture follows the destruction of Babylon the Great, which evidently occurred just before the judgments. We see the raptured church in heaven, praising God for avenging the blood of His servants. Verse 7 says: "Let us rejoice and exult and give him the glory, for the marriage of the Lamb has come, and his Bride has made herself ready."

The events of Revelation 14:6–20 appear to precede the events mentioned above and seem to be in sequential order.

> *Then I saw another angel flying directly overhead, with an eternal gospel to proclaim to those who dwell on Earth, to every nation and tribe and language and people. And he said with a loud voice, "Fear God and give him glory, because the hour of his judgment has come, and worship him who made heaven and Earth, the sea and the springs of water."*
> **Revelation 14:6–7**

We now notice John's attention is drawn to another angel proclaiming to the inhabitants of the earth "an eternal gospel to proclaim to those who dwell on Earth, to every nation and tribe and language and people." One final offer of salvation to all humanity before God's wrath is poured out, the fulfillment of Matthew 24:14: "And this gospel of the Kingdom will be proclaimed throughout the whole world as a testimony to all nations, and then the end will come."

> *Another angel, a second, followed, saying, "Fallen, fallen is Babylon the great, she who made all nations drink the wine of the passion of her sexual immorality." And another angel, a third, followed them, saying with a loud voice, "If anyone worships the Beast and its image and receives a mark on his forehead or on his hand, he also will drink the wine of God's wrath, poured full strength into the cup of his anger, and he will be tormented with fire and sulfur in the presence of the holy angels and in the presence of the Lamb. And the smoke of their torment goes up forever and ever, and they have no rest, day or night, these worshipers of the Beast and its image, and whoever receives the mark of its name."*
> **Revelation 14:8–11**

A *second angel* makes the proclamation, "Fallen, fallen is Babylon the great." Who is this "Babylon," and why is she fallen? It appears here that *Babylon falls before the time of God's wrath* (God uses an army from the north to accomplish this). We deal with this more fully in chapter 29.

A *third angel* now makes a dire warning following Babylon's demise. The warnings: do not worship the beast or his image and do not receive his mark, or you will be subject to God's wrath. It is evident the beast wants your worship, and God's wrath is focused upon those worshiping this beast. The only possibility of surviving God's wrath is to not take part in worshiping the beast or accepting his mark. There are no guarantees for those who do not accept the mark of the beast because they are now subject also to the wrath of Satan through the Antichrist. The beast and his kingdom are the focus of God's wrath.

> *This calls for patient endurance on the part of the people of God who keep his commands and remain faithful to Jesus. Then I heard a voice from heaven say, "Write this: Blessed are the dead who die in the Lord from now on." "Yes," says the Spirit, "they will rest from their labor, for their deeds will follow them."*
>
> **Revelation 14:12–13 (NIV)**

These verses are a continuation of the proclamation of the third angel. The Christians are told to be patient. Why? *The rapture has not yet occurred.* The evidence for this is that Christians will die during the time of Satan's wrath. We do not have the time fixed in Scripture as to its length, but the rapture occurs sometime during the second half of the last week of Daniel's prophecy. We are subject to Satan's wrath but not to God's wrath. Notice also that word "followed" (verses 8–9) and the phrase "from now on" (verse 13) confirm that these events are sequential.

Now we see what we were looking for: *the rapture of the church.*

> *Then I looked, and behold, a white cloud, and seated on the cloud one like a son of man, with a golden crown on his head, and a sharp sickle in his hand. And another angel came out of the temple, calling with a loud voice to*

The Rapture and the Wrath

> *him who sat on the cloud, "Put in your sickle, and reap, for the hour to reap has come, for the harvest of the Earth is fully ripe." So he who sat on the cloud swung his sickle across the Earth, and the Earth was reaped.*
>
> **Revelation 14:14–16**

Jesus is depicted as "the Son of man," sitting on a white cloud with a crown of gold ready to harvest with a sickle (verse 14). This first harvest is for the church.

We then see in the following scriptures of Revelation 14:17–20 another harvest that is for the wicked.

> *Then another angel came out of the temple in heaven, and he too had a sharp sickle. And another angel came out from the altar, the angel who has authority over the fire, and he called with a loud voice to the one who had the sharp sickle, "Put in your sickle and gather the clusters from the vine of the Earth, for its grapes are ripe." So the angel swung his sickle across the Earth and gathered the grape harvest of the Earth and threw it into the great winepress of the wrath of God. And the winepress was trodden outside the city, and blood flowed from the winepress, as high as a horse's bridle, for 1,600 stadia.*

These two events, the harvest of the church and the harvest of the wicked, begin on the same day. They have separated the righteous from the wicked by the rapture of the church. The harvest of the wicked culminates with the battle of Armageddon.

Jesus declares in Matthew 24:29–31,

> *Immediately after the tribulation of those days the sun will be darkened, and the moon will not give its light, and the stars will fall from heaven, and the powers of the heavens will be shaken. Then will appear in heaven the sign of the Son of Man, and then all the tribes of the Earth will mourn, and they will see the Son of Man coming on the clouds of heaven with power and great glory. And he will send out his angels with a loud trumpet call, and they will gather his elect from the four winds, from one end of heaven to the other.*

Rapture Does Not Occur until after the Sign

These were the signs at the removal of the sixth seal from the scroll.

Note that Jesus says, "Immediately after the tribulation of those days [referring to Satan's wrath] the sun will be darkened, and the moon will not give its light." The signs Jesus says will occur before the rapture takes place. Jesus is telling us here that Satan's wrath will occur, "But for the sake of the elect those days will be cut short" (Matthew 24:22). This places the elect (believers) in the Great Tribulation, which doesn't begin until the midpoint of the last week of Daniel's prophecy.

And he shall make a strong covenant with many for one week, and for half of the week he shall put an end to sacrifice and offering. And on the wing of abominations shall come one who makes desolate, until the decreed end is poured out on the desolator.

Daniel 9:27

Revelation 14:19–20 refers to the wrath the church does not go through; also, these verses are a short summary of the period between the beginning of God's wrath through the battle of Armageddon.

Also, in 2 Thessalonians 1:7–10, we find:

[...] and to grant relief to you who are afflicted as well as to us, when the Lord Jesus is revealed from heaven with his mighty angels In flaming fire, inflicting vengeance on those who do not know God and on those who do not obey the gospel of our Lord Jesus. They will suffer the punishment of eternal destruction, away from the presence of the Lord and from the glory of his might, when he comes on that day to be glorified in his saints, and to be marveled at among all who have believed, because our testimony to you was believed.

Verse 10 (NIV) reads: "*On the day he comes to be glorified in his holy people and to be marveled at among all those who have believed. This includes you, because you believed our testimony to you.*"

Paul's writings make it evident that punishment and rapture happen on the *same day*! Also, Paul indicates that the wicked will have no access to God during His wrath:

> *Now concerning the coming of our Lord Jesus Christ and our being gathered together to him, we ask you, brothers, not to be quickly shaken in mind or alarmed, either by a spirit or a spoken word, or a letter seeming to be from us, to the effect that the day of the Lord has come. Let no one deceive you in any way. For that day will not come, unless the rebellion comes first, and the man of lawlessness is revealed, the son of destruction, who opposes and exalts himself against every so-called god or object of worship, so that he takes his seat in the temple of God, proclaiming himself to be God.*
>
> **2 Thessalonians 2:1–4**

What about this scripture? Paul says the rapture does not occur until the "man of lawlessness is revealed": this revealing does not take place until the middle of the week when he *proclaims himself to be God*. Paul does not say the rapture occurs at this time, only that it does not occur until *after this revealing takes place*.

What Does Jesus Say about the Great Tribulation?

In Matthew 24:15–22, Jesus speaks of the Great Tribulation.

So when you see the abomination of desolation spoken of by the prophet Daniel, standing in the holy place (let the reader understand), then let those who are in Judea flee to the mountains. Let the one who is on the housetop not go down to take what is in his house, and let the one who is in the field not turn back to take his cloak. And alas for women who are pregnant and for those who are nursing infants in those days! Pray that your flight may not be in winter or on a Sabbath. For then there will be great tribulation, such as has not been from the beginning of the world until now, no, and never will be. And if those days had not been cut short, no human being would be saved. But for the sake of the elect those days will be cut short.

The *abomination of desolation* is the abomination that brings on the Great Tribulation. This occurs at the midpoint of the last week of Daniel's prophecy.

Two things emerge from this scripture:

1. There is the Great Tribulation.
2. For the elect (believers), those days will be shortened.

Mark 13:19–20 confirms this:

For in those days there will be such tribulation as has not been from the beginning of the creation that God created until now, and never will be. And if the Lord had not cut short the days, no human being would be saved. But for the sake of the elect, whom he chose, he shortened the days.

These scriptures show that the elect will go into the Great Tribulation but that it will be cut short for their sake, but not for the nonbelievers, who will remain for Satan's wrath. Satan will still have his allotted time in his attempt to defeat God, but now God is on the offensive to defeat Satan.

The Great Tribulation is not three and one-half years for the elect; it is cut short for their sake. When God cuts short the Great Tribulation for the elect by the rapture, He also seals 144,000 Jews for protection during His wrath.

The sealing of the 144,000 Jews is not accomplished until the time the church is raptured or just prior to their rapture; the idea that these 144,000 Jews are evangelists cannot be true as there is no salvation available during God's wrath.

Isaiah 2:1 says, "The Lord alone will be exalted in that day."

Points to Ponder

1. Why were the 144,000 sealed?
2. Why were the days of the Great Tribulation shortened for the elect?

29

The Fall of Babylon

Now we look at this mysterious Babylon.
- What is it?
- Where did she come from?
- Who is this prostitute?
- Why does the beast hate her?

Many questions arise from this seemingly ungodly alliance between the woman and the beast.

To get a clear understanding of this, read Revelation, chapters 17 and 18.

Ancient Babylon

This scripture must not be confused with ancient Babylon of the Old Testament, which was a very prominent city, the seat of Nebuchadnezzar's Empire, the place where Daniel dreamed his dreams, saw visions, and interpreted Nebuchadnezzar's dreams. The Babylonian Empire was responsible for the capture of Judah and the destruction of the temple in 587 BCE. Jeremiah predicted a seventy-year exile for Judah for their wickedness, after which God would punish the king of Babylon and lay it forever waste (Jeremiah 25:8–14). This occurred at the hands of the Parthians in about 130 BCE.

This Babylon the Great is not the same Babylon of the Old Testament, as it had already been destroyed. This city is called Babylon the Great because of her wickedness and must be a reference to a city corresponding to the description of her debauchery. Babylon the Great also is in a different location.

John's vision starts out at a time before the bowl judgments (Revelation 14:6–10). The angel wants John to see the punishment in store for this "great prostitute, who sits on many waters." Revelation 17:15 (NIV) reveals to us, "The waters you saw, where the prostitute sits, are peoples, multitudes, nations and languages." The *prostitute* is an entity that is worldwide in scope, not one that is local to the area of the holy land and its surrounding countries but a city with worldwide influence. Revelation 17:2 tells us that she commits adultery with kings and the inhabitants of the earth. What is going on here? It cannot be literal, can it? Let's take a good look at the situation. Israel in the Old Testament period was often chastised and punished for her prostitution. That is, for turning from God and worshiping idols. So as we look at this woman, we see idol worship involved. This worship involved a religious entity diabolically opposed to those that worship the God of Christianity. Revelation 17:6 says "that the woman was drunk with the blood of the saints, the blood of those who bore testimony to Jesus."

The Fall of Babylon

Note: idol worship is worshiping any entity, whether they are wood, gold, the sun, the moon, or anything or person that one puts before God.

We should keep several things in mind as we study this Mystery Babylon and the woman who rides the beast. See Revelation, chapter 17.

- The woman "riding" the beast seems to indicate that the woman was in control of the beast (verse 3).
- There is an unholy alliance between the woman and the beast (verse 3).
- There is much wealth in this city (verse 4).
- The woman is the city of Babylon the Great (verse 5).
- They are willing to kill God's people (verse 6).
- They hate God and all that He stands for, namely Christians and Jews (verse 14).
- The alliance between the woman (Babylon the Great) and the beast is fragile, as the beast hates her (verse 16).

Questions needing to be addressed:

- Who or what is this beast? (See chapter 12.)
- What city is this woman?
- What does this woman represent?

First, it appears this beast is the same beast that came out of the sea in Revelation 13:1, the beast of the Antichrist. At this time, we are only interested in what the beast is and its makeup in this end-time. It appears that this end-time kingdom is made up of a coalition of nations. They are a different coalition in that they are nations politically ruled by kings or presidents but controlled by Islamic Sharia law. Their motive, however, seems to be a spiritual one in that they have diabolical hatred for the Christians and Jews. Hence, they are a divided kingdom like that in the vision of Daniel's prophecy of the statue with the feet of iron and clay. It is, in reality, an unstable union of the political and spiritual.

Additionally, the woman "rides" this kingdom as if she holds the reigns. In reality, she does. See Revelation, chapter 18.

We see several things about this woman known as Babylon the Great.

- She is a home for demons (verse 2), demonically controlled.
- All nations are involved with her (verse 3).
- Kings are involved with her financially (verse 3).
- She boasts about her greatness (verse 7).
- Merchants of the earth grew rich from her (verses 11–14).
- God's people reside in her (verse 4).
- Among her cargoes: bodies and souls of men (verse 13).
- Judgment comes in one hour (verses 10, 17, 19).
- She is extremely wealthy (verses 11–14).

Now more questions arise. Where did she get all this wealth? How did she get control over this Beast?

The Fall of Babylon

When we look at what is happening here during the end-time, we realize this situation focuses on the Middle East: nations surrounding Israel, entities that hate Christians and Jews. This city, according to the evidence presented to us from the Bible, is an extremely wicked city, a city with much wealth. The evidence seems to indicate that her power over the beast kingdom was because of her wealth, apparently the financial support of many of their evil activities.

Now let us see what the Old Testament has to say concerning this "Babylon." Read Jeremiah, chapters 50 and 51.

This scripture is commonly believed to have been fulfilled in about 539 BCE. However, in looking closely at it, we find many places that are attributed to the end-time.

> *In those days and in that time, declares the Lord, iniquity shall be sought in Israel, and there shall be none. And sin in Judah, and none shall be found, for I will pardon those whom I leave as a remnant.*
>
> **Jeremiah 50:20**

This reference is to both Israel and Judah as to their guilt, and God declares, "I will pardon those whom I leave as a remnant." Israel, at the time of Jeremiah's prophecy, had long been a defeated and exiled nation. Judah was about to be exiled to Babylon, and the two nations would never again be together until they were called back to the land God promised them at the time of the end. It follows that this scripture refers to the end-time. Also, Jeremiah 50:4 (NIV) says, "'In those days, at that time,' declares the LORD, 'the people of Israel and the people of Judah together will go in tears to seek the LORD their God.'" Here again, Scripture states that both Israel and Judah will seek the Lord their God. But we know that only at the end-time will this occur. So, the information we glean from this scripture must be applied to this Mystery Babylon of Revelation 17 and 18.

Let us look at some of the other information in these chapters.

1. *Idol worship* is involved in Babylon's worship: Bel and Merodach.

> *Declare among the nations and proclaim, set up a banner and proclaim, conceal it not, and say: "Babylon is taken, Bel is put to shame, Merodach is dismayed. Her images are put to shame, her idols are dismayed."*
> **Jeremiah 50:2**

These two idols, Bel and Merodach, are one and the same. Bel, also known by various names in the Bible, is most frequently referred to as Baal. Baal worship had its origins way back in the time of Nimrod, the great-grandson of Noah. Nimrod was the builder of Babylon and, some believe, the one who started building the Tower of Babel. Baal worship was satanically inspired and involved all kinds of wicked and immoral behavior, even involving the sacrifice of children.

The Fall of Babylon

Mystery Babylon's idolatrous worship had its roots in Babylon of the Old Testament. It will come to its end when God judges her guilty of heinous acts of wickedness.

2. *Nations from the north.*

> *For behold, I am stirring up and bringing against Babylonia gathering of great nations, from the north country [...] Behold, a people comes from the north; a mighty nation and many kings are stirring from the farthest parts of the Earth.*
>
> **Jeremiah 50:9, 41**

These nations are then identified in Jeremiah 51:28: "Prepare the nations for war against her, the kings of the Medes, with their governors and deputies, and every land under their dominion."

Jeremiah also identifies Ararat, Minni, and Ashkenaz as nations summoned against Babylon in verse 51:27. Also, in Isaiah 21:2 (an oracle against Babylon), we read: "A stern vision is told to me; the traitor betrays, and the destroyer destroys. Go up, O Elam; lay siege, O Media; all the sighing she has caused I bring to an end."

3. *More information concerning* Mystery Babylon:
   a. *She resides in the desert and sits on a beast.*

> *"And he carried me away in the Spirit into a wilderness, and I saw a woman sitting on a scarlet Beast that was full of blasphemous names, and it had seven heads and ten horns" (Revelation 17:3).*

b. She is immensely wealthy.

"The woman was arrayed in purple and scarlet, and adorned with gold and jewels and pearls, holding in her hand a golden cup full of abominations and the impurities of her sexual immorality" (Revelation 17:4).

c. She has worldwide influence.

"And the angel said to me, 'The waters that you saw, where the prostitute is seated, are peoples and multitudes and nations and languages'" (Revelation 17:15).

d. She rules the kings of the earth.

"And the woman that you saw is the great city that has dominion over the kings of the Earth" (Revelation 17:18).

e. She is drunk with the blood of saints.

"And I saw the woman, drunk with the blood of the saints, the blood of the martyrs of Jesus. When I saw her, I marveled greatly" (Revelation 17:6).

f. Merchants of the earth grew rich from her.

For all nations have drunk the wine of the passion of her sexual immorality, and the kings of the Earth have committed immorality with her, and the merchants of the Earth have grown rich from the power of her luxurious living.

Revelation 18:3

g. *She is visible from the sea.*

"For in a single hour all this wealth has been laid waste." And all shipmasters and seafaring men, sailors and all whose trade is on the sea, stood far off and cried out as they saw the smoke of her burning, "What city was like the great city?"

Revelation 18:17–18

h. *In her was the blood of prophets and saints.*

"And in her was found the blood of prophets and of saints, and of all who have been slain on Earth" (Revelation 18:24).

i. *Among her cargoes—bodies and souls of men.*

"[...] and bodies and souls of men" (Revelation 18:13, NIV).

j. *She lives by many waters.*

"O you who dwell by many waters, rich in treasures, your end has come; the thread of your life is cut" (Jeremiah 51:13).

k. *The sea will rise over her.*

"The sea has come up on Babylon; she is

covered with its tumultuous waves" (Jeremiah 51:42).

l. Her marshes are set on fire.

"The fords have been seized, the marshes are burned with fire, and the soldiers are in panic" (Jeremiah 51:32).

Many scholars believe they have identified this "woman who rides the beast" ("Babylon the Great"), naming Jerusalem, Rome, New York City, and the United Nations as possible candidates. Rome is the most mentioned. Remember: Mystery Babylon must meet all the requirements as laid out in the Scriptures. You decide if they meet the criteria or not.

Please check each of these candidates against the biblical requirements.

Rome — Jerusalem — New York City — United Nations

Yes   No

Is her location in the desert? _____

Does she have worldwide influence? _____

Does she rule over the kings of the earth? _____

Is she a city? _____

Do merchants of the earth grow rich from her?

_____

Is she visible from the sea? _____

The Fall of Babylon

Are bodies and souls of men among her cargoes?

I believe we can truly say that none of the candidates' locations are in the desert. So, they all must be ruled out as possible candidates for Mystery Babylon, even though many of them meet several of the other qualifying requirements.

Where does this leave us? We must look elsewhere.

First, according to Scripture, she lies south of the nations that will attack her (see Jeremiah 51:48) since all the nations given us, as far as we can understand, are in the Middle East. Her location must then be south of these nations.

Now that we have gleaned much information concerning this Mystery Babylon, let's take a close look at her. We have learned she is an incredibly bad city with much wealth and that she has a hatred for the Christians and Jews in that she is responsible for the shedding of their blood. We know that her location is in a desert somewhere in the south of the Middle East. Much has been written concerning her as a city surrounded by seven hills or mountains, but in a closer look at the scripture, the seven hills or mountains are referring to the beast that she rides, not to Mystery Babylon herself. She resides in the desert, but the beast is comprised of seven nations with seven kings. This "beast" is much larger than a city and is controlled by the Antichrist, so the idea that Mystery Babylon must be situated among seven hills or mountains is just not correct. She is in alliance with but hated by these seven kingdoms.

Just how does this "woman," Mystery Babylon, relate to this "beast" that he hates her so much? They both seem to have the same ulterior motive behind their actions in that they both hate the Jews and the Christians and seek their eradication from this earth. Daniel gives us information concerning this "beast":

> *As for the ten horns, out of this Kingdom ten kings shall arise, and another shall arise after them; he shall be different from the former ones, and shall put down three kings. [That leaves seven.]*
>
> **Daniel 7:24**

It may be these "kings" were a thorn in the side of the Antichrist; there was just so much friction between them that this hatred arose. In any case, these two factions seem to have the same ulterior motive with differing opinions. This, however, is only speculation as there is no concrete evidence as to why the hatred.

It seems Mystery Babylon is an incredibly wealthy city. So much so that she has dealt with virtually every nation on the earth. Jeremiah tells us in 51:24, "I will repay Babylon and all the inhabitants of Chaldea before your very eyes for all the evil that they have done in Zion, declares the Lord."

The Chaldeans were people who lived in an area about 400 miles long and 100 miles wide. Chaldea comprises the southern portion of Mesopotamia, which includes Babylon and southern Iraq.

There is evidence that this Mystery Babylon is the ruling city of this Babylonia, whose kingdom will also be destroyed.

She buys and sells so much that the scriptures seem to indicate these "merchants" got rich from dealing with her. Where did she get all her wealth that she would be able to deal with these merchants, nations, and kings? I believe she became wealthy from her location in the Middle East by producing and selling oil to the nations of the earth and that this Mystery Babylon rides the "beast" because she has been the purse strings helping to support his efforts. Evidently, there will be a rift in the way things were handled between the two of them. Mystery Babylon hates the Christians and the Jews, but she also became wealthy through her dealings with them. Oil has been the driving force behind her wealth, a necessary product for world consumption. In dealing with the world, she is keeping their economy afloat. The "beast" is not interested in the economy of the world; he is interested in only one thing: world domination without Christians and Jews. His driving force is his desire to be a god and to be worshiped as a god.

This rift between the two causes the "beast" to hate her so much that he desires to crush her and bring the world to its knees economically.

"For God has put it into their hearts to carry out his purpose by being of one mind and handing over their royal power to the Beast, until the words of God are fulfilled" (Revelation 17:17).

God, instead of dealing with this situation in the time of His wrath, has allowed the beast to do it for Him as He puts the idea into the beast's heart because of his hatred for this city.

So, what is the reason the beast and this Mystery Babylon hate the Christians and Jews so much that they both want to destroy them? The Christians and Jews worship the real Creator of heaven and earth. The beast and Mystery Babylon do not worship the Creator of heaven and earth. They worship the one who wants to replace God. Allah, the god of Islam, has as his goal, through Islam, to have the entire world worship him. Allah is Satan. The Antichrist is a man possessed by Satan himself.

- Satan has always had a desire to destroy the followers of God. He has tried many times to destroy the Jews in the Old Testament.
- Haman hatched a plot to destroy the Jews, but Esther intervened, and the tables were turned.
- Daniel records conspiracies against the Jews, but again their plans were thwarted.
- Hitler had plans to rid the world of Jews through the help and advice of the Arabs. The Jews survived the Holocaust.
- Other nations throughout history have attempted to do away with the Jews, but still, the Jews survived and have reestablished their nation, Israel.

The Fall of Babylon

It would not have happened unless God had intervened in the course of history to preserve His people.

Today, Islamic fundamentalists have one desire: *to rid the world not only of Jews but Christians as well.* This last week of Daniel's prophecy is not only a political struggle but a spiritual struggle. The forces of good and the forces of evil square off. Guess who wins.

Now let's look and see if there can be found a viable candidate for the real Mystery Babylon.

1. *She is in a wilderness area.*

> *And he carried me away in the Spirit into a wilderness, and I saw a woman sitting on a scarlet Beast that was full of blasphemous names, and it had seven heads and ten horns. The woman was arrayed in purple and scarlet, and adorned with gold and jewels and pearls, holding in her hand a golden cup full of abominations and the impurities of her sexual immorality. And on her forehead was written a name of mystery: "Babylon the great, mother of prostitutes and of Earth's abominations."*
>
> **Revelation 17:3–5**

Where in the Middle East is the most likely place for Mystery Babylon's residence? The Arabian Desert seems to be the most likely place. Saudi Arabia and the countries south of her seem to be a most likely area. This area is almost entirely desert but is rich in oil.

2. *She lives by many waters.*

> *"O you who dwell by many waters, rich in treasures, your end has come; the thread of your life is cut" (Jeremiah 51:13).*

Are there any cities that would fit? Mecca, in Saudi Arabia, is a possibility, but she lies approximately forty miles from the Red Sea. She is the site of one of the holiest mosques of Islam. Saudi Arabia is a peninsula, so, in that respect, she is surrounded by "many waters." Abu Dhabi and Dubai in the United Arab Emirates are also a possibility as both are in the southern portion of the Arabian Peninsula. Abu Dhabi is located on an island in the Persian Gulf. Dubai lies on the Persian Gulf coast, approximately eighty miles to the northeast of Abu Dhabi. These three are possible locations for this Mystery Babylon.

3. *She is visible from the sea.*

> *"And all shipmasters and seafaring men, sailors and all whose trade is on the sea, stood far off and cried out as they saw the smoke of her burning, 'What city was like the great city?'" (Revelation 18:17b, 18).*

This information suggests the smoke must be able to be seen from the sea; Mecca, as noted, lies about forty miles inland. There are seven mountains between the sea and Mecca, ranging from 1,039 feet to 2,543 feet. Smoke must be visible above these mountains.

The Fall of Babylon

4. *The sea will rise over her.*

> *"The sea has come upon Babylon; she is covered with its tumultuous waves" (Jeremiah 51:42).*

As Mecca lies about forty miles inland from the sea with a mountain range between, she would be an unlikely candidate.

5. *Her marshes are set on fire.*

> *"The fords have been seized, the marshes are burned with fire, and the soldiers are in panic" (Jeremiah 51:32).*

It seems that according to the article below, this qualifies as a desert region and has marshes, qualifying Abu Dhabi and Dubai as possible candidates.

6. *The old Babylon is believed to be the location of the Tower of Babel.*

> *"We would have healed Babylon, but she cannot be healed; let us leave her and each go to his own land, for her judgment reaches to the skies, it rises as high as the clouds" (Jeremiah 51:9, NIV).*

Is Jeremiah telling us that there is another tower that reaches the sky? If so, could it be the tower built in Dubai which reaches 2,684 feet high? That is over half a mile. Dubai may well be this Mystery Babylon.

Since Dubai is an oil-rich country and controlled by

Islam, the other qualifications for Mystery Babylon are met.

I believe Dubai may be Mystery Babylon.

Note: I find no evidence of Mecca having marshes, which I believe eliminates Mecca as a candidate for Mystery Babylon, even though it has almost all the other necessary qualifications. Abu Dhabi and Dubai are not excluded based on this information.

The United Arab Emirates

- It consists of seven independent emirates, controlling an area of 51,500 square miles in the southern corner of the Arabian Peninsula.
- The country's location is in the southern corner of the Arabian Peninsula.
- Most of their coast consists of salt marshes extending far inland.
- The country is primarily a desert.

Points to Ponder

1. Who attacks Mystery Babylon?
2. Why do they attack?
3. Where do they come from?

30

The Rapture

> *And he will send out his angels with a loud trumpet call, and they will gather his elect from the four winds, from one end of heaven to the other. From the fig tree learn its lesson: as soon as its branch becomes tender and puts out its leaves, you know that summer is near. So also, when you see all these things, you know that he is near, at the very gates. Truly, I say to you, this generation will not pass away until all these things take place. Heaven and Earth will pass away, but my words will not pass away.*
>
> **Matthew 24:31–35**

Jesus often used the fig tree as a reference to the Jews. Many believe that with this reference, Jesus is indicating that the generation that sees the Jews come together as a nation "will not pass away until all these things take place."

What is a "generation"? Twenty, forty, seventy, a

hundred years? Psalm 90:10 shows us how remarkably close we are to the end: "The years of our life are seventy, or even by reason of strength eighty; yet their span is but toil and trouble; they are soon gone, and we fly away."

If we take the date that Israel became a nation in 1948, we are looking at a time around the year 2028. However, if we take the date of when Israel had total control of Jerusalem, the year would be 2047. Whichever date it is, we are remarkable close to the time of Christ's return. However, Genesis 15:13–16 tells us that a generation in God's eyes may be even longer than a hundred years.

> *Then the* L ORD *said to Abram, "Know for certain that your offspring will be sojourners in a land that is not theirs and will be servants there, and they will be afflicted for four hundred years. But I will bring judgment on the nation that they serve, and afterward they shall come out with great possessions. As for you, you shall go to your fathers in peace; you shall be buried in a good old age. And they shall come back here in the fourth generation, for the iniquity of the Amorites is not yet complete."*

What Is the Rapture?

The word "rapture" is not found in the Bible. It is man's word to describe what will happen to believers at this moment in time when Christ will come back again to resurrect His followers, whether living or dead, to be forever with Him. Many scriptures attest to this fact.

The Rapture

For this we declare to you by a word from the Lord, that we who are alive, who are left until the coming of the Lord, will not precede those who have fallen asleep. For the Lord himself will descend from heaven with a cry of command, with the voice of an archangel, and with the sound of the trumpet of God. And the dead in Christ will rise first. Then we who are alive, who are left, will be caught up together with them in the clouds to meet the Lord in the air, and so we will always be with the Lord.

1 Thessalonians 4:15–17

"For this is the will of my Father, that everyone who looks on the Son and believes in him should have eternal life, and I will raise him up on the last day" (John 6:40).

Just when this event occurs is debated by many scholars. Some will tell us the "rapture" will occur before the last week of Daniel's prophecy begins. Others disagree, contending that: it will occur in the middle of the week. Still, others say it will be at the end of Daniel's seventieth week, known as the tribulation.

The answer as to when this event will take place cannot and will not be answered by anyone other than God Himself through His Word.

The Bible alone has the answer, and it will only be revealed by extensive study of what it has to say about it. And there are many pieces to this puzzle, so we must be diligent in placing them in the right spot.

Why Is There a Rapture?

In the beginning, we were created to live forever. We were created as physical beings with the possibility to live physically forever because God placed within the garden the tree of life along with the tree of the knowledge of good and evil. Satan used his deceitfulness to convince man to partake of the fruit of the tree of the knowledge of good and evil, the fruit of which God commanded them not to eat.

> *And the LORD God commanded the man, saying, "You may surely eat of every tree of the garden, but of the tree of the knowledge of good and evil you shall not eat, for in the day that you eat of it you shall surely die."*
>
> **Genesis 2:16–17**

When man disobeyed God and ate the fruit of this tree, God cast them out of the Garden of Eden to prevent them from access to the tree of life.

> *Then the LORD God said, "Behold, the man has become like one of us in knowing good and evil. Now, lest he reach out his hand and take also of the tree of life and eat, and live forever—" therefore the LORD God sent him out from the garden of Eden to work the ground from which he was taken.*
>
> **Genesis 3:22–23**

Physically, they were still alive. Spiritually, they were dead.

The Rapture

God knew Satan would intervene in His creation of man to take care of planet Earth. He knew Satan would use lies and deception to deceive them into turning over their right to rule the earth.

So, God put in place a plan of redemption for mankind for them to return to their rightful relationship with God, a plan that would also include the defeat of Satan and imprisoning him for all eternity.

God knew Satan would do everything in his power to defeat Him, for Satan also knew that if he was unsuccessful in his efforts, he would be cast into the lake of fire.

God has revealed to us in His Word, the Bible, His plan to defeat Satan. Satan believes that if he is successful in ridding the world of Christians and Jews, he will also be successful in defeating God and be able to take over ownership of His kingdom.

Knowing Satan's plan to rid the world of Christians and Jews, God put in place a plan of escape for all who would accept His plan of redemption. His word refers to it as "gathering His elect." We call it the rapture of the church.

> *"And he will send out his angels with a loud trumpet call, and they will gather his elect from the four winds, from one end of heaven to the other" (Matthew 24:31).*

When and How Does the Rapture Occur?

Some believe the rapture occurs before the seventieth week of Daniel's prophecy begins. They believe this because they believe the first seal is the beginning of God's wrath. But is it? Let's see what the Bible will reveal about when the rapture occurs.

> *So when you see the abomination of desolation spoken of by the prophet Daniel, standing in the holy place (let the reader understand), then let those who are in Judea flee to the mountains. Let the one who is on the housetop not go down to take what is in his house, and let the one who is in the field not turn back to take his cloak. And alas for women who are pregnant and for those who are nursing infants in those days! Pray that your flight may not be in winter or on a Sabbath. For then there will be great tribulation, such as has not been from the beginning of the world until now, no, and never will be. And if those days had not been cut short, no human being would be saved. But for the sake of the elect those days will be cut short. Then if anyone says to you, "Look, here is the Christ!" or "There he is!" do not believe it. For false christs and false prophets will arise and perform great signs and wonders, so as to lead astray, if possible, even the elect. See, I have told you beforehand. So, if they say to you, "Look, he is in the wilderness," do not*

The Rapture

go out. If they say, "Look, he is in the inner rooms," do not believe it. For as the lightning comes from the east and shines as far as the west, so will be the coming of the Son of Man. Wherever the corpse is, there the vultures will gather. Immediately after the tribulation of those days the sun will be darkened, and the moon will not give its light, and the stars will fall from heaven, and the powers of the heavens will be shaken. Then will appear in heaven the sign of the Son of Man, and then all the tribes of the Earth will mourn, and they will see the Son of Man coming on the clouds of heaven with power and great glory. And he will send out his angels with a loud trumpet call, and they will gather his elect from the four winds, from one end of heaven to the other.

Matthew 24:15–31

Let's take a close look at what Jesus is revealing here in His Olivet discourse concerning the events leading up to the rapture of the church.

In verse 15, Jesus says, "When you see the *abomination of desolation*." Daniel says the event occurs in the "middle of the week," the last week of his seventy-week prophecy. It is when the Antichrist desecrates the temple by setting up an image and proclaims that he is God.

Jesus then reveals (verse 21) that there will be a Great Tribulation, a time following this abomination when Satan attacks the Jews and Christians (Revelation 12:13–17). He then goes on to tell us in verse 22 that He is going to cut short those days of tribulation for "the sake of the *elect*" (believers).

In verse 29, He begins to reveal why He cuts short the days of tribulation:
- "Immediately after the tribulation of those days,"
- "the sun will be darkened";
- "the moon will not give its light";
- "the stars will fall from heaven,"
- "and the powers of the heavens will be shaken."

Then in verses 30 and 31, He reveals what we call the rapture of the church, "Then will appear in heaven the sign of the Son of Man [...] He will send out his angels with a loud trumpet call [...] they will gather his elect from the four winds, from one end of heaven to the other."

Jesus does not reveal the wrath of God that follows the signs bringing on the day of the Lord, only what happens to the elect (believers), the rapture of the church.

Also, Daniel 12:1 tells us,

> *At that time shall arise Michael, the great prince who has charge of your people. And there shall be a time of trouble, such as never has been since there was a nation till that time. But at that time your people shall be delivered, everyone whose name shall be found written in the book.*

He states, "there shall be a time of trouble," which represents what Jesus is basically saying in Matthew 24:15, 21, that following the *abomination of desolation*, which occurs in the middle of the week, there will be a Great Tribulation. Daniel reveals a resurrection when he states, *"At that time your people shall be delivered, everyone whose name shall be found written in the book"* (Daniel 12:1).

To me, there is not a better picture of when the rapture occurs than what Jesus has shown us in His Olivet discourse. He shows us that the rapture comes at some point during the Great Tribulation by cutting this tribulation period short for the sake of the elect.

Points to Ponder

1. When does the rapture occur?
2. What happens just before the rapture of the church?

31

Before the Seventh Seal

After this I saw four angels standing at the four corners of the Earth, holding back the four winds of the Earth, that no wind might blow on Earth or sea or against any tree. Then I saw another angel ascending from the rising of the sun, with the seal of the living God, and he called with a loud voice to the four angels who had been given power to harm Earth and sea, saying, "Do not harm the Earth or the sea or the trees, until we have sealed the servants of our God on their foreheads." And I heard the number of the sealed, 144,000, sealed from every tribe of the sons of Israel: 12,000 from the tribe of Judah were sealed, 12,000 from the tribe of Reuben, 12,000 from the tribe of Gad, 12,000 from the tribe of Asher, 12,000 from the tribe of Naphtali, 12,000 from the tribe of Manasseh, 12,000 from the tribe of Simeon, 12,000 from the tribe of Levi, 12,000 from the tribe of Issachar, 12,000 from the tribe of Zebulun, 12,000 from the tribe of Joseph, 12,000 from the tribe of Benjamin were sealed. After this I looked, and behold, a great multitude that no one could number, from every nation, from all tribes and peoples and languages, standing before the throne and before the Lamb, clothed in white robes, with palm branches in their hands, and crying out with a loud voice, "Salvation belongs to our God who sits on the throne, and to the Lamb!" And all the angels were standing around the throne and around the elders and the four living creatures, and they fell on their faces before the throne and worshiped God, saying, "Amen! Blessing and glory and wisdom and thanksgiving and honor and power and might be to our God forever and ever! Amen." Then one of the elders addressed me, saying, "Who are these, clothed in white robes, and from where have they come?" said to him, "Sir, you know." And he said to me, "These are the ones coming out of the great tribulation. They have washed their robes and made them white in the blood of the Lamb. Therefore they are before the throne of God, and serve him day and night in his temple; and he who sits on the throne will shelter them with his presence. They shall hunger no more, neither thirst anymore; the sun shall not strike them, nor any scorching heat. For the Lamb in the midst of the throne will be their shepherd, and he will guide them to springs of living water, and God will wipe away every tear from their eyes."

Revelation 7:1–17

Before the Seventh Seal

Something needed to be done before God would pour out His wrath upon mankind:
- People needed protection
- The sealing of the 144,000
- The rapture of the church

It is interesting to note that God called these 144,000 Jews "servants."

The church is raptured following the sealing of the 144,000 Jews. The Jews are seen as the "servants of God." I believe they accept Jesus as their Savior immediately after the rapture. However, they could have been Christians, but God chose to seal them for them to physically reestablish the Jewish population on the earth after Satan is defeated.

Verse 9 is a picture of the rapture taking place at some point during the last three and one-half years of Daniel's prophecy. We noticed the souls of the saints that died up to the events of the fifth seal's removal were residing under the altar, a holding place for the saints awaiting the rapture.

"They cried out with a loud voice, 'O Sovereign Lord, holy and true, how long before you will judge and avenge our blood on those who dwell on the Earth?'" (Revelation 6:10).

It is quite clear that God's wrath had not yet been poured out *and* that the rapture had not yet occurred.

We now see the raptured saints "standing before the throne and before the Lamb." The rapture of the church clears the way for God's wrath to begin.

I do not know just when these seal openings occur, but my understanding is that their removal involves the entrance of a deceiving entity. This entity, I believe, was Muhammad, who was the deceiver leading to the establishment of the Muslim empire. His claim was, "God is one, and he doesn't need a son" (a half-truth, the same tactic Satan used in the Garden of Eden).

Seal one has already been removed from the scroll!

The seventh seal will be removed, revealing God's wrath at some point during the last half of the seventieth week, just after the rapture and the sealing of the 144,000 Jews.

The idea conveyed by many that the 144,000 Jews were sealed to be evangelists during the time of God's wrath is just not true. There is a real problem here. These 144,000 Jews were sealed just before God's wrath. The Scriptures tell us that the temple in heaven was closed while God's wrath was being poured out. The temple was closed; there was no salvation available to those under God's wrath. It is just an assumption that these Jews were evangelists.

Points to Ponder
1. What does the seventh seal's removal reveal?
2. The saints are in heaven. What happened?

32

Seventh Seal

There were seven seals sealing the scroll. Each seal had a condition that must occur before the seal could be removed. Once all the seals are removed, the inside contents of the scroll will be revealed, showing what God has planned for His cleansing planet Earth of evil and the 1,000-year imprisonment of Satan.

> *When the Lamb opened the seventh seal, there was silence in heaven for about half an hour. Then I saw the seven angels who stand before God, and seven trumpets were given to them. And another angel came and stood at the altar with a golden censer, and he was given much incense to offer with the prayers of all the saints on the golden altar before the throne, and the smoke of the incense, with the prayers of the saints, rose before God from the hand of the angel. Then the angel took the censer and filled it with fire from the altar and threw it on the Earth, and there were peals of thunder, rumblings, flashes of lightning, and an Earthquake.*
>
> **Revelation 8:1–5**

Revelation 8 reveals the opening of the seventh seal, which allows the writings on the inside of the scroll to be viewed. I believe they reveal God's judgments that will result in His cleansing the world of evil and setting up the millennial reign of Christ.

Points to Ponder

1. What happened when the seventh seal was removed?
2. What does the inside of the scroll reveal?

33
God's Wrath

After God's wrath on the earth's inhabitants begins, salvation will not be available until after the battle of Armageddon. God has sealed 144,000 Jews for their protection during this period of God's judgments. There is no evidence that people repented of their evil ways during this time. Revelation 15:8 tells of the unavailability of God's temple during God's wrath: "And the sanctuary was filled with smoke from the glory of God and from his power, and *no one could enter the sanctuary until the seven plagues of the seven angels were finished.*"

Verse 8 is the last verse of Revelation 15 before the angels are told to pour out their seven bowl judgments. Hebrews 8 and 9 tell us that Jesus serves as our mediator in the sanctuary in heaven. The closing of the sanctuary, as indicated in Revelation 15:8, reveals to us that the Mediator (Jesus, our great High Priest) is not available until the opening of the sanctuary following God's wrath. Revelation 11:19 speaks of when the temple again opens following the seventh trumpet.

The saints will have been raptured before the sanctuary is closed because our High Priest will be unavailable, as He (Jesus, the "Lion of the tribe of Judah") has other things to attend to: the pouring out of His wrath on the earth.

Old Testament scriptures confirm that spiritual darkness reigns during the day of the Lord. The day of the Lord begins as a dark day with no light in it. This light referred to in the Old Testament is a spiritual light. The New Testament tells us there is light from the sun and the moon during the events of God's wrath. That will be a physical light.

Amos 5:18–20 says,

> *Woe to you who desire the day of the Lord! Why would you have the day of the Lord? It is darkness, and not light, as if a man fled from a lion, and a bear met him, or went into the house and leaned his hand against the wall, and a serpent bit him. Is not the day of the Lord darkness, and not light, and gloom with no brightness in it?*

> *The great day of the Lord is near, near and hastening fast; the sound of the day of the Lord is bitter; the mighty man cries aloud there. A day of wrath is that day, a day of distress and anguish, a day of ruin and devastation, a day of darkness and gloom, a day of clouds and thick darkness.*
>
> **Zephaniah 1:14–15**

God's Wrath

"I must work the works of him that sent me, while it is day: the night cometh, when no man can work" (John 9:4, KJV).

The rest of mankind, who were not killed by these plagues, did not repent of the works of their hands nor give up worshiping demons and idols of gold and silver and bronze and stone and wood, which cannot see or hear or walk, nor did they repent of their murders or their sorceries or their sexual immorality or their thefts.
Revelation 9:20–21

They still *did not repent* because the Holy Spirit was not working in them, which would have led them to repentance. Salvation was not available since the church (the light of the world) was raptured before God's wrath began. God was not going to leave the church on the earth while our Mediator was unavailable in the temple because it was closed during His wrath being poured out on evil.

It appears Revelation 10:8–11:13 is an insert for information, not a part of the sixth trumpet. We need to find a place for this part of the puzzle. The passage refers to events happening near the middle of this last prophetic week culminating just before the sounding of the seventh trumpet.

Revelation 11:15b reveals when the seventh trumpet is blown: "The Kingdom of the world has become the Kingdom of our Lord and of his Christ, and he shall reign forever and ever."

The seventh bowl judgment involving the battle of Armageddon is over, and Jesus has conquered His enemies. The seventh trumpet sounding is the announcement of His victory and what follows. The saints will take part in this battle. The church has been battling evil ever since its birth. God will not deny the church in participating in this victory over evil.

> *But that in the days of the trumpet call to be sounded by the seventh angel, the mystery of God would be fulfilled, just as he announced to his servants the prophets. [...] Then the seventh angel blew his trumpet, and there were loud voices in heaven, saying, "The Kingdom of the world has become the Kingdom of our Lord and of his Christ, and he shall reign forever and ever." And the twenty-four elders who sit on their thrones before God fell on their faces and worshiped God, saying, "We give thanks to you, Lord God Almighty, who is and who was, for you have taken your great power and begun to reign. The nations raged, but your wrath came, and the time for the dead to be judged, and for rewarding your servants, the prophets and saints, and those who fear your name, both small and great, and for destroying the destroyers of the Earth." Then God's temple in heaven was opened, and the ark of his covenant was seen within his temple. There were flashes of lightning, rumblings, peals of thunder, an Earthquake, and heavy hail.*
>
> **Revelation 10:7, 11:15–19**

God's Wrath

Revelation 12–14 is an interlude between the trumpet judgments and the Bowl judgments. The trumpet judgments and the bowl judgments are the same judgments. The trumpets announce the judgments, and the bowls are the judgments. A careful study of the two reveals that the bowls and the trumpet judgments are the same. This will be confirmed as we continue our study.

Let's look at the scriptures revealing God's wrath.

Revelation, chapter 6, reveals the opening of the first six seals on the scroll. Seal seven (revealing the judgments awaiting the wicked of the earth) has yet to be opened. Seal six reveals the signs, the announcement that *the day of the Lord* is about to begin.

"The sun shall be turned to darkness, and the moon to blood, *before* the great and awesome day of the Lord comes" (Joel 2:31).

> *But in those days, after that tribulation, the sun will be darkened, and the moon will not give its light, and the stars will be falling from heaven, and the powers in the heavens will be shaken. And then they will see the Son of Man coming in clouds with great power and glory. And then he will send out the angels and gather his elect from the four winds, from the ends of the Earth to the ends of heaven.*
> **Mark 13:24–27**

Here we see that there are signs *after* the tribulation and *before* the Lord's day begins and *before* the rapture of the saints, as indicated by Mark's Gospel. It is also recorded in the Gospels of Matthew and Luke in their Olivet discourse passages.

What "tribulation" is Mark referring to (verse 24)? It is the same tribulation brought on by the events revealed by the first five seals, as recorded in Revelation 6, and by the desires and efforts of the Antichrist.

As mentioned before, the trumpet and bowl judgments are, in reality, one and the same.

Before these judgments occur, there are two other events we need to look at, as recorded in Revelation 7.

1. The sealing of the 144,000 Jews. Why was it necessary to seal them?
2. The removal of the church, the rapture, where the Christians are called to meet Christ in the clouds.

The sealing needed to happen as they would need protection from the wrath of God known as the Lord's day and protection from the Antichrist.

The 144,000 Jews (the "remnant") would need protection during the time of divine judgment (God's judgment on unbelievers and the wicked), as through them, God would reestablish the Jewish community. I believe they were not Christians when the rapture occurred. If they were, they would have been part of the church and raptured. They most likely accepted Christ as their Savior immediately following the rapture but before God's wrath. The idea they were 144,000 evangelists is simply not true, as salvation was not available during God's wrath. There is evidence later in Revelation that they were indeed followers of Christ.

God's Wrath

Points to Ponder

1. Was salvation available during God's wrath?
2. What happens before God's wrath is poured out?

34

The Trumpets

The trumpet and bowl judgments are the wrath of God poured out on planet Earth. Both seem to have the same elements in them. Could they be the same? Let's look at the Scriptures and see what it has to say concerning trumpets.

> *The Lord spoke to Moses, saying, "Make two silver trumpets. Of hammered work you shall make them, and you shall use them for summoning the congregation and for breaking camp. [...] But when the assembly is to be gathered together, you shall blow a long blast, but you shall not sound an alarm. [...] And when you go to war in your land against the adversary who oppresses you, then you shall sound an alarm with the trumpets, that you may be remembered before the Lord your God, and you shall be saved from your enemies. On the day of your gladness also, and at your appointed feasts and at the beginnings of your months, you shall blow*

the trumpets over your burnt offerings and over the sacrifices of your peace offerings. They shall be a reminder of you before your God: I am the Lord your God."
Numbers 10:1–2, 7, 9–10

Seven priests shall bear seven trumpets of rams' horns before the ark. On the seventh day you shall march around the city seven times, and the priests shall blow the trumpets. And when they make a long blast with the ram's horn, when you hear the sound of the trumpet, then all the people shall shout with a great shout, and the wall of the city will fall down flat, and the people shall go up, everyone straight before him.
Joshua 6:4–5

"Sing praises to the Lord with the lyre, with the lyre and the sound of melody! With trumpets and the sound of the horn make a joyful noise before the King, the Lord!" (Psalm 98:5–6).

"And if he sees the sword coming upon the land and blows the trumpet and warns the people" (Ezekiel 33:3).

These scriptures are representative of all the Scriptures concerning the trumpets being blown. As can be seen, the trumpets are used only for the purpose of calling the people to worship, battle, call an alarm, and for singing praises to the Lord. The trumpet blows with different sounds for the various purposes of their blowing. The trumpets were never used as a vehicle for judgment, only for announcements. In this end-time setting, the trumpets were only used for announcing the bowl judgments. *The bowls carried the judgments announced by the sounding of the trumpet.* In this end-time, it is possible that the sounding of the trumpet will be heard by all. Announcing to all that God is about to pour out another judgment on the earth.

We are going to discover in our study the trumpet and bowl judgments are, in reality, one and the same. The trumpet sounds to announce another judgment.

> *Then I saw another sign in heaven, great and amazing, seven angels with seven plagues, which are the last, for with them the wrath of God is finished. And I saw what appeared to be a sea of glass mingled with fire—and also those who had conquered the Beast and its image and the number of its name, standing beside the sea of glass with harps of God in their hands. And they sing the song of Moses, the servant of God, and the song of the Lamb, saying, "Great and amazing are your deeds, O Lord God the Almighty! Just and true are your ways, O King of the nations! Who will not fear, O Lord, and glorify your name? For you alone are holy. All nations will come and worship you, for your righteous acts have been revealed." After this I looked, and the sanctuary of the tent of witness in heaven*

was opened, and out of the sanctuary came the seven angels with the seven plagues, clothed in pure, bright linen, with golden sashes around their chests. And one of the four living creatures gave to the seven angels seven golden bowls full of the wrath of God who lives forever and ever, and the sanctuary was filled with smoke from the glory of God and from his power, and no one could enter the sanctuary until the seven plagues of the seven angels were finished.
Revelation 15:1–8

Now compare Revelation 7:9:

After this I looked, and behold, a great multitude that no one could number, from every nation, from all tribes and peoples and languages, standing before the throne and before the Lamb, clothed in white robes, with palm branches in their hands.

Moreover, Revelation 15:2:

And I saw what appeared to be a sea of glass mingled with fire and also those who had conquered the Beast and its image and the number of its name, standing beside the sea of glass with harps of God in their hands.

It appears that in both cases, before Judgment begins, an event occurs that looks as if it could be the raptured saints in heaven.

Also, notice in both scriptures preceding the judgments

The Trumpets

that there is another event similar in nature.

"And the smoke of the incense, with the prayers of the saints, rose before God from the hand of the angel" (Revelation 8:4).

Note: Revelation 15:8 above says, "no one could enter the sanctuary," suggesting that *salvation* is not available to those under God's judgments. See also verse 11:19, where after the seventh trumpet sounded, the temple again opens for the availability of salvation.

> *Then God's temple in heaven was opened, and the ark of his covenant was seen within his temple. There were flashes of lightning, rumblings, peals of thunder, an Earthquake, and heavy hail.*
> **Revelation 11:19**

If the trumpet and bowl judgments are different, why is it that the opening of the temple occurred with the blast of the seventh trumpet and then closed before the first bowl judgment?

The revelation to John reveals an interesting hint as to the correlation between the trumpet and bowl judgments. The scriptures concerning the bowl judgments follow the scriptures about the trumpet judgments. However, the closing of the temple happens prior to the passages dealing with the bowl judgments. See Revelation 15:8 above.

The opening of God's sanctuary following the sounding of the seventh trumpet in Revelation 11:19 places the bowl judgments entirely within the trumpet soundings.

When John saw the angels blowing the trumpets, he saw what was happening. When John saw the angels pouring out their bowls, he could see what caused the judgments.

First Judgment

The first angel blew his trumpet.

> *Now the seven angels who had the seven trumpets prepared to blow them. The first angel blew his trumpet, and there followed hail and fire, mixed with blood, and these were thrown upon the Earth. And a third of the Earth was burned up, and a third of the trees were burned up, and all green grass was burned up.*
>
> **Revelation 8:6–7**

The first bowl was poured out.

> *Then I heard a loud voice from the temple telling the seven angels, "Go and pour out on the Earth the seven bowls of the wrath of God." So the first angel went and poured out his bowl on the Earth, and harmful and painful sores came upon the people who bore the mark of the Beast and worshiped its image.*
>
> **Revelation 16:1–2**

Most people looking at the trumpet and bowl judgments believe that they are administered as two separate judgments. But a closer look reveals a very

The Trumpets

close relationship between each trumpet sounding and its corresponding bowl judgment. Let's investigate.

The first angel blew his trumpet, and there followed "hail and fire, mixed with blood and these were thrown upon the Earth." My question is: Who or what caused it to hail? All this first angel did was blow his trumpet, and "hail and fire, mixed with blood were thrown upon the Earth." Together they show what was thrown on the earth, who threw it, and what the "hail and fire mixed with blood" caused. Putting these two together gives us a better picture of what happened with this first judgment.

The angel blew his trumpet, announcing to the angel holding the bowl to pour out the first plague of God's wrath: "hail and fire, mixed with blood, and these were thrown upon the Earth." It caused one-third of the earth, one-third of the trees, and all the grass to be burned up. And on the people, "harmful and painful sores came upon the people who bore the mark of the Beast and worshiped its image."

Second Judgment

The second angel blew his trumpet.

> *The second angel blew his trumpet, and something like a great mountain, burning with fire, was thrown into the sea, and a third of the sea became blood. A third of the living creatures in the sea died, and a third of the ships were destroyed.*
>
> **Revelation 8:8–9**

Again, we see the trumpet blowing and "and something like a great mountain, burning with fire, was thrown into the sea." But it doesn't reveal who threw the "mountain" into the sea. To see the results of what happened, we must wait until the second bowl judgment to see what caused this event to occur.

The second bowl was poured out.

> "The second angel poured out his bowl into the sea, and it became like the blood of a corpse, and every living thing died that was in the sea" (Revelation 16:3).

You may say yes, but the trumpet says, "A third of the living creatures in the sea died, and a third of the ships were destroyed," and the second bowl reveals that "every living thing died that was in the sea." My belief is that when John was shown the blowing of the second trumpet, he was only shown the beginning of the plague, while the bowl showed the entire effect of the plague.

Third Judgment

The third angel blew his trumpet.

> The third angel blew his trumpet, and a great star fell from heaven, blazing like a torch, and it fell on a third of the rivers and on the springs of water. The name of the star is Wormwood. A third of the waters became wormwood, and many people died from the water, because it had been made bitter.
>
> **Revelation 8:10–11**

The Trumpets

The third bowl was poured out.

> *The third angel poured out his bowl into the rivers and the springs of water, and they became blood. And I heard the angel in charge of the waters say, "Just are you, O Holy One, who is and who was, for you brought these judgments. For they have shed the blood of saints and prophets, and you have given them blood to drink. It is what they deserve!" And I heard the altar saying, "Yes, Lord God the Almighty, true and just are your judgments!"*
>
> **Revelation 16:4–7**

The third judgment shows *both trumpet and bowl were on the rivers and springs of water.* Same judgment, two viewpoints. The bowl judgment does not record it as limited to one-third of the rivers and springs. The effects of the two judgments, however, were essentially the same as the third trumpet, stating that the rivers and the springs of water became bitter, while the third bowl states that God has given them blood to drink.

Fourth Judgment

The fourth angel blew his trumpet.

> *The fourth angel blew his trumpet, and a third of the sun was struck, and a third of the moon, and a third of the stars, so that a third of their light might be darkened, and a third of the day might be kept from shining, and likewise a third of the night. Then I looked,*

> *and I heard an eagle crying with a loud voice as it flew directly overhead, "Woe, woe, woe to those who dwell on the Earth, at the blasts of the other trumpets that the three angels are about to blow!"*
>
> **Revelation 8:12–13**

The fourth bowl was poured out.

> *The fourth angel poured out his bowl on the sun, and it was allowed to scorch people with fire. They were scorched by the fierce heat, and they cursed the name of God who had power over these plagues. They did not repent and give him glory.*
>
> **Revelation 16:8–9**

Both the fourth trumpet and bowl judgments deal with the sun, moon, and stars. The fourth trumpet judgment is that their light would be "kept from shining." The fourth bowl judgment reveals the effect of the sun to "scorch people" with its heat. Note that it says, "They did not repent and give him glory." There is a reason they did not repent, the light of the world (spiritual light) had been removed, so there was no working of the Holy Spirit to convict them of their sin. Also, the temple in heaven was closed; access was not available. An eagle warns of three more woes to come upon the earth.

Fifth Judgment

The fifth angel blew his trumpet.

And the fifth angel blew his trumpet, and I saw a star fallen from heaven to Earth, and he was given the key to the shaft of the bottomless pit. He opened the shaft of the bottomless pit, and from the shaft rose smoke like the smoke of a great furnace, and the sun and the air were darkened with the smoke from the shaft. Then from the smoke came locusts on the Earth, and they were given power like the power of scorpions of the Earth. They were told not to harm the grass of the Earth or any green plant or any tree, but only those people who do not have the seal of God on their foreheads. They were allowed to torment them for five months, but not to kill them, and their torment was like the torment of a scorpion when it stings someone. And in those days people will seek death and will not find it. They will long to die, but death will flee from them. In appearance the locusts were like horses prepared for battle: on their heads were what looked like crowns of gold; their faces were like human faces, their hair like women's hair, and their teeth like lions' teeth; they had breastplates like breastplates of iron, and the noise of their wings was like the noise of many chariots with horses rushing into battle. They have tails and stings like scorpions, and their power to hurt people for five months is in their tails. They have as

king over them the angel of the bottomless pit. His name in Hebrew is Abaddon, and in Greek he is called Apollyon. The first woe has passed; behold, two woes are still to come.
Revelation 9:1–12

The fifth bowl was poured out.

The fifth angel poured out his bowl on the throne of the Beast, and its Kingdom was plunged into darkness. People gnawed their tongues in anguish and cursed the God of heaven for their pain and sores. They did not repent of their deeds.
Revelation 16:10–11

It is evident from the information of this trumpet and bowl judgment that God's wrath focuses mainly on the beast and his kingdom, but the 144,000 Jews sealed by God are exempt from this plague.

The vision John received of locusts seemed to be difficult for John to express. John verbalized what he saw; that is, he described them to the best of his ability. Remember: John was in heaven seeing heavenly revelations of what, in reality, was an event on the earth. These "locusts" John saw were the best description he was able to make of them.

What were they? They were real but, probably, very small. They came out of the smoke of the abyss in hoards. John described them the best he could. These insects, perhaps actual locusts, might have been an ancient species

The Trumpets

trapped in this bottomless pit where God confined fallen angels to be let loose at this time.

Whatever position is taken as to what they were, they were real, and the hurt they put on those not sealed by God was real.

Also, note the fifth bowl judgment only announces where the bowl was poured out. There is no mention of what caused their pain and sores. However, Revelation 16:11 indicates they cursed God for their pain and sores. The pain and sores arise out of the announcement of the fifth trumpet (Revelation 9:3–5), tying the fifth trumpet and bowl judgments together.

Sixth Judgment

The sixth angel blew his trumpet.

> *Then the sixth angel blew his trumpet, and I heard a voice from the four horns of the golden altar before God, saying to the sixth angel who had the trumpet, "Release the four angels who are bound at the great river Euphrates." So the four angels, who had been prepared for the hour, the day, the month, and the year, were released to kill a third of mankind. The number of mounted troops was twice ten thousand times ten thousand; I heard their number. And this is how I saw the horses in my vision and those who rode them: they wore breastplates the color of fire and of sapphire and of sulfur, and the heads of the horses were like lions' heads, and fire and*

> smoke and sulfur came out of their mouths. By these three plagues a third of mankind was killed, by the fire and smoke and sulfur coming out of their mouths. For the power of the horses is in their mouths and in their tails, for their tails are like serpents with heads, and by means of them they wound. The rest of mankind, who were not killed by these plagues, did not repent of the works of their hands nor give up worshiping demons and idols of gold and silver and bronze and stone and wood, which cannot see or hear or walk, nor did they repent of their murders or their sorceries or their sexual immorality or their thefts.
>
> **Revelation 9:13–21**

The sixth bowl was poured out.

> *The sixth angel poured out his bowl on the great river Euphrates, and its water was dried up, to prepare the way for the kings from the east. And I saw, coming out of the mouth of the dragon and out of the mouth of the Beast and out of the mouth of the false prophet, three unclean spirits like frogs. For they are demonic spirits, performing signs, who go abroad to the kings of the whole world, to assemble them for battle on the great day of God the Almighty.*
>
> **Revelation 16:12–14**

It seems abundantly evident from the trumpet and bowl judgments that they are one and the same: two angels with

The Trumpets

two different commands, affecting the same outcome.

The sixth trumpet sounded (9:13), and the sixth bowl judgment was poured out, as instructed, on the great river, the Euphrates (16:12). This was the only time the angel who blew a trumpet was ever told to do something different than announcing that a judgment was coming. He was told to "release the four angels who are bound at the great river Euphrates." The angel holding the bowl judgment was instructed to *pour out his bowl on the great river Euphrates.* Evidently, the Euphrates River needed to be dried up *before* the four angels could be released, indicating to us that the trumpet and bowl judgments are one and the same.

It appears the angels released by the sixth trumpet for this day were released on a particular day and hour, already fixed by God as to when this event should occur. Their release will lead to the destruction of one-third of mankind and the gathering of their forces of evil for the battle of Armageddon.

The number of two hundred million troops is real. The vision of the horses and the armament they fought with cannot be explained, but there may be the involvement of nuclear weapons. The destruction was immense as one-third of mankind died. The Antichrist amassed his hoard along with the armies of Gog already in Israel and those of the kings of the east. Jesus, in Revelation 17:14, has gathered His army in preparation for the battle. Antichrist is defeated in the valley of Armageddon along with his army, the armies of Gog, and the kings of the east, amounting to 200,000,000 soldiers.

Imagine what the flow of blood in the violent death of 200,000,000 warriors would be? If only two pints of blood bled from each, there would be 50,000,000 gallons of blood flowing. Revelation 14:20 reveals this blood flowed for 160 miles with a depth to the horse's bridle. We do not know the width of the flow. It may seem preposterous, but when a calculation of the possibilities is made, one finds that one cubic foot equals 7.481 gallons. A stream 160 miles long would be five feet high. The math works.

After Revelation 9, there is an interlude between the blowing of the first six trumpets and the blowing of the seventh trumpet. The seventh trumpet resumes in chapter 11, verse 14. This interlude does not mean there is a time difference between the sixth and seventh trumpets. John receives other information pertinent to the seventh trumpet or prior to the seventh trumpet and bowl judgments.

The Seven Thunders

John, after the vision of the sixth trumpet judgment, was given another vision that was relevant to it, as we notice in:

> *Then I saw another mighty angel coming down from heaven, wrapped in a cloud, with a rainbow over his head, and his face was like the sun, and his legs like pillars of fire. He had a little scroll open in his hand. And he set his right foot on the sea, and his left foot on the land, and called out with a loud*

The Trumpets

voice, like a lion roaring. When he called out, the seven thunders sounded. And when the seven thunders had sounded, I was about to write, but I heard a voice from heaven saying, "Seal up what the seven thunders have said, and do not write it down." And the angel whom I saw standing on the sea and on the land raised his right hand to heaven and swore by him who lives forever and ever, who created heaven and what is in it, the Earth and what is in it, and the sea and what is in it, that there would be no more delay, but that in the days of the trumpet call to be sounded by the seventh angel, the mystery of God would be fulfilled, just as he announced to his servants the prophets. Then the voice that I had heard from heaven spoke to me again, saying, "Go, take the scroll that is open in the hand of the angel who is standing on the sea and on the land." So I went to the angel and told him to give me the little scroll. And he said to me, "Take and eat it; it will make your stomach bitter, but in your mouth it will be sweet as honey." And I took the little scroll from the hand of the angel and ate it. It was sweet as honey in my mouth, but when I had eaten it my stomach was made bitter. And I was told, "You must again prophesy about many peoples and nations and languages and kings."

Revelation 10:1–11

Following the scriptures revealing the sixth trumpet judgment, there is an interlude placed in the Scripture.

John receives more information that culminates at this point in the dialog Jesus reveals to John.

What did these seven thunders say? We do not know because John is told not to write it down. Is there any inference or knowledge that we can glean from this portion of Scripture? I believe there is, though not with absolute certainty. Remember: we do not want to assume anything.

- The thunders were uttered between the sixth and seventh trumpet soundings.
- In verse 6 of the narration, the angel declares, "There will be no more delay!"
- Verse 7 declares, "But in the days when the seventh angel is about to sound his trumpet, the mystery of God will be accomplished, just as he announced to his servants the prophets."

It appears that these seven thunders pertain to the events that take place between the sixth and seventh trumpet judgments. What information, if any, can we find that would take place between the sixth and seventh judgments?

The sixth trumpet judgment reveals events that will lead up to, but not include, the battle of Armageddon. Could it be that the thunders revealed to John just how God was going to defeat Satan at this final battle of the age? We do not know, but that it is an exceedingly good possibility as the seventh trumpet sounding seems to declare.

> *The seventh angel sounded his trumpet, and there were loud voices in heaven, which said:*

The Trumpets

"The Kingdom of the world has become the Kingdom of our Lord and of his Christ, and he will reign for ever and ever."

Revelation 11:15

John is then told to take the scroll and eat it: "It will make your stomach bitter, but in your mouth it will be sweet as honey" (Revelation 10:9).

- The battle was victorious for Jesus, "sweet as honey."
- But the bloodshed to gain the victory was *sour.*

Then John was told, "You must prophesy again about many peoples, nations, languages, and kings."

Seventh Judgment

The seventh angel blew his trumpet.

The second woe has passed; behold, the third woe is soon to come. Then the seventh angel blew his trumpet, and there were loud voices in heaven, saying, "The Kingdom of the world has become the Kingdom of our Lord and of his Christ, and he shall reign forever and ever." And the twenty-four elders who sit on their thrones before God fell on their faces and worshiped God, saying, "We give thanks to you, Lord God Almighty, who is and who was, for you have taken your great power and begun to reign. The nations raged, but your wrath came, and the time for the dead to be judged, and for rewarding your servants, the prophets and saints, and those who fear your name, both small and great, and for destroying the destroyers of the Earth." Then God's temple in heaven was opened, and the ark of his covenant was seen within his temple. There were flashes of lightning, rumblings, peals of thunder, an Earthquake, and heavy hail.

Revelation 11:14–19

Notice verse 14 above states that the "second woe has passed" and that a "third woe is soon to come." Then when the seventh trumpet is blown, there are voices coming from heaven that state, "The Kingdom of the world has become the Kingdom of our Lord and of his Christ, and he shall reign forever and ever." This indicates to me that the battle of Armageddon is over and that Christ and His army have won. This means the seventh week of Daniel's prophecy is also over, and we are entering into a time of restoration. Satan has been defeated, and then we can understand why verse 19 above says, "Then God's temple in heaven was opened, and the ark of his covenant was seen within his temple," which seems to indicate that God's wrath is complete. And yet there is no evidence of a third woe until after this statement. All the seventh-trumpet scriptures tell us is, "There were flashes of lightning, rumblings, peals of thunder, an Earthquake, and heavy hail." Let us find out if there is information forthcoming with evidence from the seventh bowl judgment.

The seventh bowl was poured out.

The Trumpets

> *The seventh angel poured out his bowl into the air, and a loud voice came out of the temple, from the throne, saying, "It is done!" And there were flashes of lightning, rumblings, peals of thunder, and a great Earthquake such as there had never been since man was on the Earth, so great was that Earthquake. The great city was split into three parts, and the cities of the nations fell, and God remembered Babylon the great, to make her drain the cup of the wine of the fury of his wrath. And every island fled away, and no mountains were to be found. And great hailstones, about one hundred pounds each, fell from heaven on people; and they cursed God for the plague of the hail, because the plague was so severe.*

Revelation 16:17–21

The terminology of both the trumpet and bowl judgments seems to indicate these two judgments do indeed end at the same point in the future. Verse 15 of this last trumpet judgment says, "The Kingdom of the world has become the Kingdom of our Lord and of his Christ," indicating that this judgment finishes the events of God's wrath, that the battle of Armageddon is finished, and that Jesus was victorious. Verse 17 of this last bowl judgment says, "[…] and a loud voice came out of the temple, from the throne, saying, 'It is done!'" Again, indicating that this last battle has been won.

However, the scriptures that follow this declaration may seem to question that statement, as there is evidently a worldwide plague of events taking place (the third woe). See verses 18–21 of the seventh bowl judgment.

What I believe this scripture is telling us is that, indeed, Satan has been defeated at the battle of Armageddon and that his army of two hundred million soldiers perished. The battle was a territorial battle focused upon the nation of Israel with participants from many of the neighboring countries.

How did that victory get won? We don't know; however, there is some evidence that I believe will shed some light on it. As noted at the end of the sixth trumpet, John was given a vision of seven thunder judgments. John saw what was going to happen but was not permitted to tell us.

The biblical evidence seems to indicate:

- The trumpet sounded, and the angel poured out his bowl judgment, which released the seven thunder judgments, which I believe were God's battle plan of attacking Satan's army at Armageddon.
- Following this victory, the sanctuary in heaven was opened under the trumpet sounding (verse 19). The events then described under the seventh bowl judgment were then poured out on the entire world.

Revelation 15:8 says, "And the sanctuary was filled with smoke from the glory of God and from his power, and no one could enter the sanctuary until the seven plagues of the seven angels were finished."

The Trumpets

This statement, made before the Judgments began, tells us, "And no one could enter the sanctuary until the seven plagues of the seven angels were finished," meaning salvation was not available during God's wrath. Verse 19 of the seventh trumpet judgment tells us the temple was again open, indicating the angels had completed their job of pouring out God's wrath to destroy evil.

It appears that the battle of Armageddon, as described under the seventh bowl judgment, occurred before the blowing of the seventh judgment as the seventh trumpet announced the temple (sanctuary) in heaven was again open. The blowing of the seventh trumpet also announces, "The Kingdom of the world has become the Kingdom of our Lord and of his Christ, and he shall reign forever and ever" (verse 15).

If you yet believe the trumpet and bowl judgments are two separate judgments, then I have this question for you: If these seven trumpet and seven bowl judgments were different judgments, then why was the temple closed immediately before the seven bowl judgments but opened following the seven trumpet judgments? It just doesn't make sense.

Following the scripture above stating, "It is done," is when the final woe is poured out. It appears that God has opened His temple in heaven to allow salvation to those who will accept it. What seems to occur according to the Scriptures is that God took this short period of time to prepare His earth for His millennial kingdom.

Points to Ponder
1. Are the trumpet and bowl judgments the same?
2. What about the availability of salvation during these judgments?

35

After the Battle

After the battle of Armageddon is a time of cleanup for the victors, those living in Israel will be given jobs to do, namely burying the dead bodies from the battle.

Ezekiel 39:12–15 says,

> *For seven months the house of Israel will be burying them, in order to cleanse the land. All the people of the land will bury them, and it will bring them renown on the day that I show my glory, declares the Lord God. They will set apart men to travel through the land regularly and bury those travelers remaining on the face of the land, so as to cleanse it. At the end of seven months they will make their search. And when these travel through the land and anyone sees a human bone, then he shall set up a sign by it, till the buriers have buried it in the Valley of Hamon-gog.*

It seems evident that the strife of war is over as the residents of Israel try to resume their everyday life. They begin to pick up the pieces and cleanse the land. The enemy has been defeated, and there is no more fear of their evil ambitions.

In Ezekiel 39:21–29, God tells us,

> *And I will set my glory among the nations, and all the nations shall see my judgment that I have executed, and my hand that I have laid on them. The house of Israel shall know that I am the Lord their God, from that day forward. And the nations shall know that the house of Israel went into captivity for their iniquity, because they dealt so treacherously with me that I hid my face from them and gave them into the hand of their adversaries, and they all fell by the sword. I dealt with them according to their uncleanness and their transgressions, and hid my face from them. "Therefore thus says the Lord God: Now I will restore the fortunes of Jacob and have mercy on the whole house of Israel, and I will be jealous for my holy name. They shall forget their shame and all the treachery they have practiced against me, when they dwell securely in their land with none to make them afraid, when I have brought them back from the peoples and gathered them from their enemies' lands, and through them have vindicated my holiness in the sight of many nations. Then they shall know that I am the Lord their God, because I sent them into exile among the nations and then assembled them into their own land. I will leave none of them*

After the Battle

> *remaining among the nations anymore. And I will not hide my face anymore from them, when I pour out my Spirit upon the house of Israel, declares the Lord God."*

God has declared in verse 22 above that: "The house of Israel shall know that I am the Lord their God, from that day forward."

God tells us that Israel will finally acknowledge the Lord as their God. From this point forward, according to the scriptures above, God will call all those who had not previously returned to Israel to return now.

God is now ready to establish His kingdom on the earth, the 1000-year millennial reign of Christ.

Isaiah 65:16–25 records,

> *So that he who blesses himself in the land shall bless himself by the God of truth, and he who takes an oath in the land shall swear by the God of truth; because the former troubles are forgotten and are hidden from my eyes. "For behold, I create new heavens and a new Earth, and the former things shall not be remembered or come into mind. But be glad and rejoice forever in that which I create; for behold, I create Jerusalem to be a joy, and her people to be a gladness. I will rejoice in Jerusalem and be glad in my people; no more shall be heard in it the sound of weeping and the cry of distress. No more shall there be in it an infant who lives but a few days, or an old man who does not fill out his days, for*

the young man shall die a hundred years old, and the sinner a hundred years old shall be accursed. They shall build houses and inhabit them; they shall plant vineyards and eat their fruit. They shall not build and another inhabit; they shall not plant and another eat; for like the days of a tree shall the days of my people be, and my chosen shall long enjoy the work of their hands. They shall not labor in vain or bear children for calamity, for they shall be the offspring of the blessed of the Lord, and their descendants with them. Before they call I will answer; while they are yet speaking I will hear. The wolf and the lamb shall graze together; the lion shall eat straw like the ox, and dust shall be the serpent's food. They shall not hurt or destroy in all my holy mountain," says the Lord.

These scriptures give us a glimpse into what the millennial kingdom will be like. Satan will have been banished to the abyss for a thousand years. He will be brought back again after the thousand years are over, but during the thousand years, there will be peaceful bliss. It appears from this reading that sin is nonexistent as the planet seems to have been put back into a state like the Garden of Eden.

After the thousand years, Satan will be loosed. His goal is to deceive people in his desire to replace God. The question as to why Satan must be loosed may be recorded in Revelation 20:2–3:

After the Battle

> *And he seized the dragon, that ancient serpent, who is the devil and Satan, and bound him for a thousand years, and threw him into the pit, and shut it and sealed it over him, so that he might not deceive the nations any longer, until the thousand years were ended. After that he must be released for a little while.*

We are not given the reasons why he must be loosed, only that he is loosed for a *short time*. However, the reason seems to be an obvious one. Those born during the millennial reign must be given the opportunity to choose who they want to serve, as up to this point in the millennial kingdom, there was no choice available to those born during this time. Satan may be loosed for this purpose only.

> *And when the thousand years are ended, Satan will be released from his prison and will come out to deceive the nations that are at the four corners of the Earth, Gog and Magog, to gather them for battle; their number is like the sand of the sea. And they marched up over the broad plain of the Earth and surrounded the camp of the saints and the beloved city, but fire came down from heaven and consumed them, and the devil who had deceived them was thrown into the lake of fire and sulfur where the Beast and the false prophet were, and they will be tormented day and night forever and ever.*
>
> **Revelation 20:7–10**

As can be seen, Satan goes *across the breadth of the earth* to deceive, gathering his forces as he surrounds *the camp of God's people*. In the end, God destroys them with fire, and the devil is thrown into the lake of fire.

So ends Satan's efforts to usurp God's kingdom. He is forever imprisoned in the lake of fire, where he is *tormented day and night forever and ever.*

36

Putting the Pieces Together

We have looked at the individual pieces to this end-time puzzle. The pieces were many as they were scattered throughout the Bible. Some were simple to understand where in this puzzle they belonged. Others were more difficult as they were only meant to be understood at the time of the end. We must be very close, as their meaning is now being revealed.

We have seen almost all the players involved in this picture. We saw the makeup of this end-time "beast." How he started, who he involved, his last "beast empire," and what he did to try to accomplish his goal of world domination and to be worshipped as God. This "beast," of course, is Satan, who hated God's chosen people, the Jews, and Christians.

We see John as he was called into heaven to bear witness to the events leading up to Christ's return to establish His kingdom on the earth.

These events begin with the Lamb removing the first seal from the scroll, leading to a countdown to the "covenant of peace" that begins the last seven years of Daniel's prophecy. I believe Satan himself came to a man named Muhammad, disguised as an "angel of light" with false claims that would ultimately lead him to start a false religion claiming that God is one and He doesn't need a son. I believe this false religion is Islam and Satan is its god (known as "Allah" to millions). Muhammad bought into this lie and began teaching it to all who would listen. We probably will not know the exact moment the rest of the seals have been or will be removed from the scroll.

We can know, however, just when this last week begins and ends. It begins when this "covenant of peace," a seven-year document, is signed by Satan's beast kingdom, its leader, and Israel (only if it has been made public).

God's Word reveals that Israel will be living in a time of relevant peace. This peace, I believe, occurs only when this "covenant" is signed, allowing Israel to rebuild a temple of worship, allowing them to sacrifice burnt offerings to God again. This temple is completed, and sacrifices begin 265 days into this agreement (see chart in chapter 16). Once their sacrificial worship begins, they truly believe that peace has finally arrived in Israel. But, in their dismay, after 965 days from the opening of the temple, disaster strikes.

Gog, with his evil intentions, invades Israel for the purpose of looting them of everything that has value. This occurs thirty days before the absolute middle of this final week of Daniel's prophecy (215 days to the start of sacrifices, 965 days of sacrifice until Gog invades = 1,230 days), leaving thirty days till the middle of the week.

Several things occur rapidly during this thirty-day period, ending on day 1,260, the middle of the week. These events are not necessarily in order.

- Michael, God's archangel, has been fighting Satan in the spiritual realm of heaven. He defeats Satan and casts him and his angels down to the earth.
- Satan, once cast out of heaven, will possess the Antichrist. From this point on, it will be Satan himself leading the activities of his beast kingdom.
- The Antichrist (Satan) marches into Jerusalem under the guise of protecting Israel.
- The false prophet sets up an image of the Antichrist and demands its worship.
- The Antichrist (now possessed) marches into the temple and commits the "abomination of desolation," declaring that he is God.
- God sends His two witnesses to work against the efforts of the Satan-possessed Antichrist, giving them 1,260 days to perform their duties.
- God limits the Antichrist to 1,260 days till his demise (the end of the week).
- Jesus declares this to be a time of Great Tribulation.

Following the Antichrist's declaration of being God, he goes after those Jews living in Judea with a desire to annihilate them from the face of the earth. Failing to do so because of God's protection, he turns his attention to the

Christians. His activities cause the Lamb to open seal four with seal five closely following. During this period, the false prophet sets up a system demanding a seal be placed in your right hand or on your forehead for you to be able to buy or sell anything.

The conditions will become so bad and the deceptions so intense that Jesus sends the signs that announce His coming is imminent; it is then that the angel opens the sixth seal.

- 144,000 Jews sealed
- Angels proclaiming the Gospel in midair
- Babylon the Great is destroyed
- The rapture of the church
- Temple in heaven is closed; no salvation is available

God's wrath begins:

- Judgment 1. The first angel poured out his bowl on the earth, and harmful and painful sores came upon the people who bore the mark of the beast and worshipped its image.
- Judgment 2. The second angel poured out his bowl into the sea, and it became like the blood of a corpse, and every living thing died that was in the sea.
- Judgment 3. The third angel poured out his bowl into the rivers and springs of water, and they became blood.
- Judgment 4. The fourth angel poured out his bowl on the sun, and it was allowed to scorch people with fire.

Putting the Pieces Together

- Judgment 5. The fifth angel poured out his bowl on the throne of the beast, and its kingdom was plunged into darkness.
- Judgment 6. The sixth angel poured out his bowl on the river Euphrates, and its water was dried up to prepare the way for the kings from the east. And they assembled them at the place that in the Hebrew is called Armageddon.
- Two witnesses are killed and then resurrected.
- Seven thunders occur.
- Battle of Armageddon is fought; the Antichrist and the false prophet are cast alive into the lake of fire.
- Gog is buried in the hills of Israel.
- Satan is cast into the abyss.
- Judgment 7. The seventh angel pours out his bowl into the air, and a loud voice comes out of the temple, from the throne, saying, "It is done." The seventh week is over; Satan has been defeated and locked away for 1,000 years.
- The temple in heaven is opened; salvation is again available.
- The third woe occurs—the intense activities required for the restoration of the earth.
- The 1,000-year millennial reign of Christ begins.

God's End-Time Puzzle

EVENTS OF THE ENDTIME

SEAL 1	THE DECEIVER ARRIVES	The Deceiver - Seal most likely removed following the Advent of Islam	Rev. 6:1-2	The First Seal is opened prior to the Seven year Covenant
SEAL 2	PEACE TAKEN FROM EARTH	Peace taken from the Earth - May have been removed because of Islam's jihad activities.	Rev. 6:3-4	
SEAL 3	ECONOMIC CHAOS	Economic Chaos - Close to removal if not already removed.	Rev. 6:5-6	

A SEVEN YEAR COVENANT IS SIGNED — Israel and Antichrist sign a Seven Year Covenant

Gog Invades Israel - Ezekiel 38:1 - 39:29

The Midpoint of the Last Seven Years — Covenant is Broken

	SATAN CAST OUT OF HEAVEN	Rev. 12:1-10	The Great Tribulation Begins
	SATAN POSSESSES THE ANTICHRIST	Rev. 13 1-8	
	SATAN PURSUES ISRAEL - ISRAEL FLEES UNDER GOD' PROTECTION	Rev. 12:13-17	
	SATAN TURNS HIS FOCUS TOWARD THE CHRISTIANS WORLWIDE	Rev. 12:17	SATAN'S
	FALSE PROPHET EMPOWERED	Rev. 13:11-18	
	MARK OF THE BEAST INSTITUTED	Rev. 13:11-18	
	TWO WITNESSES COMMISSIONED BY GOD	Rev. 11:1-14	
SEAL 4	WAR, FAMINE, PLAGUE — War, Famine and Plague	Rev. 67-8	W R A T H
SEAL 5	MARTYRDOM - The focus of the Antichrist and Islam will be on destroying the Christians in Muslum Countries.	Rev. 6:9-11	
SEAL 6	**THE SIGNS - SUN, MOON, AND STARS** Rev. 6:12-17		
	LOOK UP FOR YOUR REDEMPTION DRAWETH NIGH.	Luke 21:28	
	THE 144,000 SEALED	Rev.7:1-8	
	ANGELS PROCLAIMING THE GOSPEL IN MID-AIR	Rev. 14:6-7	
	BABYLON THE GREAT IS DESTROYED	Rev. 14:8	
	THE CHURCH MEETS CHRIST IN THE CLOUDS	Matt. 24:30-31	

Putting the Pieces Together

	THE RAPTURE OF THE CHURCH - Tribulation shortened for the Believers.		1 Thes. 4:16-17 Matt. 24:22
SEAL 7	THE WRATH OF GOD BEGINS		
	TEMPLE IN HEAVEN IS CLOSED - NO SALVATION AVAILABLE		Rev. 15:8
JUDGMENT 1	harmful and painful sores came upon the people who bore the mark of the beast and worshiped its image		Rev. 8:7; 16:2
JUDGMENT 2	The second angel poured out his bowl into the sea, and it became like the blood of a corpse, and every living thing died that was in the sea.		Rev. 8:8; 16:3
JUDGMENT 3	⁴The third angel poured out his bowl into the rivers and the springs of water, and they became blood. 6 For they have shed the blood of saints and prophets,		Rev. 8:10-11 16:4-6
JUDGMENT 4	The fourth angel poured out his bowl on the sun, and it was allowed to scorch people with fire.		Rev. 8:12-13 16:8-9
JUDGMENT 5	The fifth angel poured out his bowl on the throne of the beast, and its kingdom was plunged into darkness.		Rev. 9:1-12 16:10-11
JUDGMENT 6	¹²The sixth angel poured out his bowl on the great river Euphrates, and its water was dried up, to prepare the way for the kings from the east. 16 And they assembled them at the place that in Hebrew is called Armageddon.		Rev. 9:13-21 16:12-16
	TWO WITNESSES KILLED, THEN RESURRECTED		Rev. 11:11
	SEVEN THUNDERS		Rev. 10:1-7
	Battle of Armageddon Fought - Antichrist and False Profit Cast Alive into the Lake of Fire, Gog Buried in the Hills of Israel - Satan Cast into the Abyss		Rev. 19:19-20
JUDGMENT 7	The seventh angel poured out his bowl into the air, and a loud voice came out of the temple, from the throne, saying, "It is done!"		Rev. 11:15-19 16:17-21
	TEMPLE IN HEAVEN IS OPENED - SALVATION AGAIN AVAILABLE		
	THE MILLENIAL KINGDOM BEGINS AND LASTS FOR 1000 YEARS		Rev. 20:1-6

GOD'S WRATH

CHURCH HAS BEEN RAPTURED AND IS IN HEAVEN

About the Author

It was in 1935 that I first saw the light of day, but not until the summer of 1950 that I made my commitment to follow the Lord Jesus Christ as my Savior. I was always interested in reading and studying the end-time. It was still later, in the seventies, that my passion really grew when I received a book called *The Late Great Planet Earth* by Hal Lindsay. It seemed I bought almost every book on the end-time no matter what position they took, whether a pre-, mid-, or post-tribulation position. It seemed they all had valid arguments for their position. Also, I was confused as to what the truth really was concerning the timing of how these end-time events would take place.

It was during this turmoil in my mind that I decided to throw all my end-time learning aside and study only the Bible to see if I could come to the truth as to the timing of these events. It was difficult but necessary to cast aside some of the concepts I had accepted as truth. The intensity of my study began to be rewarded as it seemed the Lord began revealing to me the truth. I took the position that all the truth of the end-time would be revealed in the Bible. I did not need to consult any commentary or book as to what others believed; the Bible would have the answer to all the questions. I remember times in the struggle when I needed to find the answer to my questions. I would lie awake at night wondering about how certain events would occur. Many times, after falling asleep, I would suddenly wake up with a clear understanding of how they all fit in place. After many years of study, I believe I have found the truth as to how the pieces of this puzzle fit in place. The result is this book I call *God's End-Time Puzzle: Letting Scripture Speak for Itself*. It will always be the right answer to any question you might have.

I, William Edmondson, am the husband of Janice, my wife of sixty-six years. We have three children: Steven, Karen, and Kathy—all follow Jesus as their Savior.

GOD'S
End-Time
PUZZLE

LETTING SCRIPTURE SPEAK FOR ITSELF

William C. Edmondson

TRILOGY
PROFESSIONAL PUBLISHING MEETS POWERFUL PROMOTION

A wholly owned subsidiary of TBN

God's End-time Puzzle: Letting Scripture Speak for Itself

Trilogy Christian Publishers A Wholly Owned Subsidiary of Trinity Broadcasting Network

2442 Michelle Drive Tustin, CA 92780

Copyright © 2022 by William C. Edmondson

Unless otherwise indicated, all Scripture quotations are from The Holy Bible, English Standard Version®), copyright © 2001 by Crossway Bibles, a publishing ministry of Good News Publishers. Used by permission. All rights reserved. Scripture quotations marked NIV are taken from the Holy Bible, New International Version®, NIV®. Copyright © 1973, 1978, 1984, 2011 by Biblica, Inc.™ Used by permission of Zondervan. All rights reserved worldwide. www.zondervan.com. The "NIV" and "New International Version" are trademarks registered in the United States Patent and Trademark Office by Biblica, Inc.™ Scripture quotations marked NKJV are taken from the New King James Version®. Copyright © 1982 by Thomas Nelson. Used by permission. All rights reserved. Scripture quotations marked KJV are taken from the King James Version of the Bible. Public domain.

No part of this book may be reproduced, stored in a retrieval system, or transmitted by any means without written permission from the author. All rights reserved. Printed in the USA.

Rights Department, 2442 Michelle Drive, Tustin, CA 92780.

Trilogy Christian Publishing/TBN and colophon are trademarks of Trinity Broadcasting Network.

Cover design by: Trilogy

For information about special discounts for bulk purchases, please contact Trilogy Christian Publishing.

Trilogy Disclaimer: The views and content expressed in this book are those of the author and may not necessarily reflect the views and doctrine of Trilogy Christian Publishing or the Trinity Broadcasting Network.

Manufactured in the United States of America

10 9 8 7 6 5 4 3 2 1

Library of Congress Cataloging-in-Publication Data is available.

ISBN: 978-1-64773-271-4

E-ISBN: 978-1-64773-272-1